The Poetry Of Letitia Elizabeth Landon - Volume 1

Letitia Elizabeth Landon was born on 14 August 1802 in Chelsea, London. A precocious child she had her first poem published is 1820 using the single 'L' as her marker. The following year her first volume appeared and sold well. She published a further two poems that same year with just the initials 'L.E.L." It provided the basis for much intrigue.

She became the chief reviewer of the Gazette and published her second collection, The Improvisatrice, in 1824.

By 1826, rumours began to circulate that she had had affairs. For several years they continued to circulate until she broke off an engagement when her betrothed, upon further investigation, found them to be unfounded. Her words reflect the lack of trust she felt "The mere suspicion is dreadful as death"

On June 7th 1838 she married George Maclean, initially in secret, and a month later they sailed to Cape Coast. However the marriage proved to be short lived as on October 15th Letitia was found dead, a bottle of prussic acid in her hand.

Her reputation as a poet diminished until fairly recently; her work felt to be simplistic and too simply constructed. However when put into context it is more rightly seen as working on many levels and meanings as was needed for those more moral times.

Index Of Poems

Scenes In London I – Piccadilly by Letitia Elizabeth Landon

The sun is on the crowded street,
It kindles those old towers;
Where England's noblest memories meet,
Of old historic hours.

Vast, shadowy, dark, and indistinct,
Tradition's giant fane,
Whereto a thousand years are linked,
In one electric chain.

So stands it when the morning light
First steals upon the skies;
And shadow'd by the fallen night,
The sleeping city lies.

It stands with darkness round it cast,
Touched by the first cold shine;
Vast, vague, and mighty as the past,
Of which it is the shrine.

'Tis lovely when the moonlight falls
Around the sculptured stone
Giving a softness to the walls,
Like love that mourns the gone.

Then comes the gentlest influence
The human heart can know,
The mourning over those gone hence
To the still dust below.

The smoke, the noise, the dust of day,
Have vanished from the scene;
The pale lamps gleam with spirit ray
O'er the park's sweeping green.

Sad shining on her lonely path,
The moon's calm smile above,
Seems as it lulled life's toil and wrath
With universal love.

Past that still hour, and its pale moon,
The city is alive;
It is the busy hour of noon,
When man must seek and strive.

The pressure of our actual life
Is on the waking brow;
Labour and care, endurance, strife,
These are around him now.

How wonderful the common street,
Its tumult and its throng,
The hurrying of the thousand feet
That bear life's cares along.

How strongly is the present felt,

With such a scene beside;
All sounds in one vast murmur melt
The thunder of the tide.

All hurry on—none pause to look
Upon another's face:
The present is an open book
None read, yet all must trace.

The poor man hurries on his race,
His daily bread to find;
The rich man has yet wearier chase,
For pleasure's hard to bind.

All hurry, though it is to pass
For which they live so fast—
What doth the present but amass,
The wealth that makes the past.

The past is round us—those old spires
That glimmer o'er our head;
Not from the present is their fires,
Their light is from the dead.

But for the past, the present's powers
Were waste of toil and mind;
But for those long and glorious hours
Which leave themselves behind.

Scenes In London II - Oxford Street
Life in its many shapes was there,
The busy and the gay;
Faces that seemed too young and fair
To ever know decay.

Wealth, with its waste, its pomp, and pride,
Led forth its glittering train;
And poverty's pale face beside
Asked aid, and asked in vain.

The shops were filled from many lands,
Toys, silks, and gems, and flowers;
The patient work of many hands,
The hope of many hours.

Yet, mid life's myriad shapes around
There was a sigh of death;
There rose a melancholy sound,
The bugle's wailing breath.

They played a mournful Scottish air,
That on its native hill
Had caught the notes the night-winds bear
From weeping leaf and rill.

'Twas strange to hear that sad wild strain
Its warning music shed,
Rising above life's busy train,
In memory of the dead.

There came a slow and silent band
In sad procession by:
Reversed the musket in each hand,
And downcast every eye.

They bore the soldier to his grave;
The sympathyzing crowd
Divided like a parted wave
By some dark vessel ploughed.

A moment, and all sounds were mute,
For awe was over all;
You heard the soldier's measured foot,
The bugle's wailing call.
The gloves were laid upon the bier,
The helmet and the sword,
The drooping war-horse followed near,
As he, too, mourned his lord.
Slowly—I followed too—they led
To where a church arose,
And flung a shadow o'er the dead,
Deep as their own repose.
Green trees were there—beneath the shade
Of one, was made a grave;
And there to his last rest was laid
The weary and the brave.

They fired a volley o'er the bed
Of an unconscious ear;
The birds sprang fluttering overhead,
Struck with a sudden fear.

All left the ground, the bugles died
Away upon the wind;
Only the tree's green branches sighed
O'er him they left behind.

Again, all filled with light and breath,
I passed the crowded street—
Oh, great extremes of life and death,
How strangely do ye meet!

Scenes In London III - The Savoyard In Grosvenor Square

He stands within the silent square,
That square of state, of gloom;
A heavy weight is on the air,
Which hangs as o'er a tomb.

It is a tomb which wealth and rank
Have built themselves around—
The general sympathies have shrank
Like flowers on high dry ground.

None heed the wandering boy who sings,
An orphan though so young;
None think how far the singer brings
The songs which he has sung.

None cheer him with a kindly look,
None with a kindly word;
The singer's little pride must brook
To be unpraised, unheard.

At home their sweet bird he was styled,
And oft, when days were long,
His mother called her favourite child
To sing her favourite song.

He wanders now through weary streets,
Till cheek and eye are dim;
How little sympathy he meets,

Sudden his dark brown cheek grows bright
His dark eyes fill with glee,
Covered with blossoms snowy-white,
He sees an orange tree.

No more the toil-worn face is pale,
Nor faltering step is sad;
He sees his distant native vale,
He sees it, and is glad.

He sees the squirrel climb the pine,
The doves fly through the dell,
The purple clusters of the vine;
He hears the vesper-bell.

His heart is full of hope and home,
Toil, travel, are no more;
And he has happy hours to come
Beside his father's door.

Oh, charm of natural influence!
But for thy lovely ties,
Never might the world-wearied sense
Above the present rise.

Blessed be thy magic everywhere,
Oh Nature, gentle mother;
How kindlier is for us thy care,
Than ours is for each other.

Scenes In London IV - The City Churchyard

I pray thee lay me not to rest
Among these mouldering bones;
Too heavily the earth is prest
By all these crowded stones.

Life is too gay—life is too near
With all its pomp and toil;
I pray thee do not lay me here,
In such a world-struck soil.

The ceaseless roll of wheels would wake
The slumbers of the dead;
I cannot bear for life to make
Its pathway o'er my head.

The flags around are cold and drear,
They stand apart, alone;
And no one ever pauses here,
To sorrow for the gone.

No: lay me in the far green fields
The summer sunshine cheers;
And where the early wild flower yields
The tribute of its tears.

Where shadows the sepulchral yew,
Where droops the willow tree,
Where the long grass is filled with dew
Oh! make such grave for me!
And passers-by, at evening's close,
Will pause beside the grave,
And moralize o'er the repose
They fear, and yet they crave.

Perhaps some kindly hand may bring
Its offering to the tomb;
And say, As fades the rose in spring,
So fadeth human bloom.

But here there is no kindly thought
To soothe, and to relieve;
No fancies and no flowers are brought,
That soften while they grieve.

Here Poesy and Love come not
It is a world of stone;
The grave is bought—is closed—forgot!
And then life hurries on.

Sorrow and beauty—nature—love
Redeem man's common breath;
Ah! let them shed the grave above—
Give loveliness to death.

Revenge

Ay gaze upon her smile;
Seem as you drank the very air
Her breath perfumed the while:
And wake for her the gifted line,
That wild and witching lay,
And swear your heart is as a shrine,
That only owns her sway.

'Tis well: I am revenged at last,
Mark you that scornful cheek,
The eye averted as you pass'd,
Spoke more than words could speak.

Ay, now by all the bitter tears
That I have shed for thee,
The racking doubts, the burning fears,
Avenged they well may be

By the nights pass'd in sleepless care,
The days of endless woe;
All that you taught my heart to bear,
All that yourself will know.

I would not wish to see you laid
Within an early tomb;
I should forget how you betray'd,
And only weep your doom:

But this is fitting punishment,
To live and love in vain,
Oh my wrung heart, be thou content,
And feed upon his pain.

Go thou and watch her lightest sigh,
Thine own it will not be;
And bask beneath her sunny eye,
It will not turn on thee.

'Tis well: the rack, the chain, the wheel,
Far better hadst thou proved;
Ev'n I could almost pity feel,
For thou art nor beloved.

On An Engraving Of Hindoo Temples
Little the present careth for the past,
Too little—'tis not well!
For careless ones we dwell
Beneath the mighty shadow it has cast.

Its blessings are around our daily path,
We share its mighty spoil,
We live on its great toil,
And yet how little gratitude it hath.

Look on these temples, they were as a shrine
From whence to the far north
The human mind went forth,
The moral sunshine of a world divine—

That inward world which maketh of our clay
Its temporary home;
From whence those lightnings come,
That kindle from a far and better day.

The light that is of heaven shone there the first
The elements of art,
Mankind's diviner part;
There was young science in its cradle nurst.

Mighty the legacies by mind bequeathed,
For glorious were its pains
Amid those giant fanes,
And mighty were the triumphs it achieved
A woman's triumph mid them is imprest
One who upon the scroll Flung the creative soul,

Disdainful of life's flowers and of its rest.
Vast was the labour, vast the enterprise,
For she was of a race
Born to the lowest place,
Earth-insects, lacking wings whereon to rise.

How must that youthful cheek have lost its bloom,

How many a dream above
Of early hope and love
Must that young heart have closed on like a tomb.

Such throw life's flowers behind them, and aspire
To ask the stars their lore
And from each ancient store
Seek food to stay the mind's consuming fire.

Her triumph was complete and long, the chords
She struck are yet alive;
Not vainly did she strive
To leave her soul immortal on her words.

A great example has she left behind,
A lesson we should take,
Whose first task is to wake
The general wish to benefit our kind.

Our sword has swept o'er India; there remains
A nobler conquest far,
The mind's ethereal war,
That but subdues to civilize its plains.

Let us pay back the past, the debt we owe,
Let us around dispense
Light, hope, intelligence,
Till blessings track our steps where'er we go.

O England, thine be the deliverer's meed,
Be thy great empire known
By hearts made all thine own,
By thy free laws and thy immortal creed.

Amelioration and the Future, Man's Noble Tasks
Fall, fall, ye mighty temples to the ground:
Not in your sculptured rise
Is the real exercise Of human nature's brightest power found.

'Tis in the lofty hope, the daily toil,
'Tis in the gifted line,
In each far thought divine,
That brings down Heaven to light our common soil.

'Tis in the great, the lovely, and the true;
'Tis in the generous thought,
Of all that man has wrought,
Of all that yet remains for man to do.

The Nizam's Daughter

She is yet a child in years,
Twelve springs are on her face,
Yet in her slender form appears
The woman's perfect grace.
Her silken hair, that glossy black,
But only to be found
There, or upon the raven's back,
Falls sweeping to the ground.

'Tis parted in two shining braids
With silver and with gold,
And one large pearl by contrast aids
The darkness of each fold.
And for she is so young, that flowers
Seem natural to her now,
There wreaths the champac's snowy showers
Around her sculptured brow.

Close to her throat the silvery vest
By shining clasps is bound,
Scarce may her graceful shape be guest,
Mid drapery floating round.
But the small curve of that veined throat,
Like marble, but more warm,
The fairy foot and hand denote
How perfect is the form.

Upon the ankle and the wrist
There is a band of gold,
No step by Grecian fountain kiss'd,
Was of diviner mould.
In the bright girdle round her waist,
Where the red rubies shine,
The kandjar's glittering hilt is placed,
To mark her royal line.

Her face is like the moonlight pale,
Strangely and purely fair,
For never summer sun nor gale
Has touched the softness there.
There are no colours of the rose,
Alone the lip is red;
No blush disturbs the sweet repose
Which o'er that cheek is shed.
And yet the large black eyes, like night,
Have passion and have power;
Within their sleepy depths is light
For some wild wakening hour.
A world of sad and tender dreams
'Neath those long lashes sleep,

A native pensiveness that seems
Too still and sweet to weep.

Of such seclusion know we nought:
Yet surely woman here
Grows shrouded from all common thought,
More delicate and dear.
And love, thus made a thing apart,
Must seem the more divine,
When the sweet temple of the heart
Is a thrice-veiled shrine.

The Orphan

Alone, alone! - no other face
Wears kindred smile, kindred line;
And yet they say my mother's eyes.
They say my father's brow, is mine;
And either had rejected to see
The other's likeness in my face,
But now it is a stranger's eye,
That finds some long forgotten trace.

I heard them name my father's death,
His home and tomb alike the wave;
And I was early taught to weep,
Beside my youthful mother's grave.
I wish I could recall one look,
But only one familiar tone;
If I had aught of memory,
I should not feel so all alone.

My heart is gone beyond the grave,
In search of love I cannot find,
Till I could fancy soothing words
Are whisper'd by the ev'ning wind:
I gaze upon the watching stars,
So clear, so beautiful above,
Till I could dream they look on me
With something of an answering love.

My mother! does thy gentle eye
Look from those distant stars on me?
Or does the wind at ev'ning bear
A message to thy child from thee?
Dost thou pine for me, as I pine
Again a parent's love to share?
I often kneel beside thy grave,
And pray to be a sleeper there.
The vesper bell! - 'tis eventide,
I will not weep, but I will pray:

God of the fatherless, 'tis Thou
Alone canst be the orphan's stay!
Earth's meanest flower, heaven's mightiest star,
Are equal to their Maker's love.
And I can say, 'Thy will be done,'
With eyes that fix their hopes above.

The Pilgrim
Vain folly of another age,
This wandering over earth,
To find the peace by some dark sin
Banish'd our household hearth.

On Lebanon the dark green pines
Wave over sacred ground,
And Carmel's consecrated rose
Springs from a hallow'd mound.

Glorious the truth they testify,
And blessed is their name;
But even in such a sacred spot,
Are sin and woe the same.

O pilgrim! with each toilsome step,
Vain every weary day;
There is no charm in soil or shrine,
To wash thy guilt away.

Return, with prayer and tear, return
To those who weep at home;
To dry their tears will more avail,
Than o'er a world to roam.

There's hope for one who leaves with shame,
The guilt that lured before;
Remember, He who said, 'Repent,'
Said also, 'Sin no more.'
Return, and in thy daily round
Of duty and of love,
Thou best wilt find that patient faith
Which lifts the soul above.

In ev'ry innocent prayer, each child
Lisps at his father's knee: -
If thine has been to teach that prayer,
There will be hope for thee.

There is a small white church, that stands
Beside thy father's grave,
There kneel and pour those earnest prayers,

That sanctify and save.
Around thee draw thine own home-ties,
And, with a chasten'd mind,
In meek well-doing seek that peace,
No wandering will find.

In charity and penitence,
Thy sin will be forgiven: -
Pilgrim, the heart is the true shrine,
Whence prayers ascend to Heaven.

The Poor

Few, save the poor, feel for the poor:
The rich know not how hard
It is to be of needful food
And needful rest debarred.

Their paths are paths of plenteousness,
They sleep on silk and down;
And never think how heavily
The weary head lies down.

They know not of the scanty meal,
With small pale faces round;
No fire upon the cold, damp hearth
When snow is on the ground.

They never by the window lean,
And see the gay pass by;
Then take their weary task again,
But with a sadder eye

The Power of Words

'Tis a strange mystery, the power of words!
Life is in them, and death. A word can send
The crimson colour hurrying to the cheek.
Hurrying with many meanings; or can turn
The current cold and deadly to the heart.
Anger and fear are in them; grief and joy
Are on their sound; yet slight, impalpable:
A word is but a breath of passing air.

The Reply Of The Fountain

How deep within each human heart,
A thousand treasured feelings lie;
Things precious, delicate, apart,
Too sensitive for human eye.

Our purest feelings, and our best,
Yet shrinking from the common view;
Rarely except in song exprest,
And yet how tender, and how true!

They wake, and know their power, when eve
Flings on the west its transient glow;
Yet long dark shadows dimly weave
A gloom round some green path below.

Who dreams not then—the young dream on
Life traced at hope's delicious will;
And those whose youth of heart is gone,
Perhaps have visions dearer still.

They rise, too, when expected least,
When gay yourself, amid the gay,
The heart from revelry hath ceased
To muse o'er hours long past away.

And who can think upon the past
And not weep o'er it as a grave?
How many leaves life's wreath has cast!
What lights have sunk beneath the wave!

But most these deep emotions rise
When, drooping o'er our thoughts alone,
Our former dearest sympathies
Come back, and claim us for their own.

Such mood is on the maiden's mind
Who bends o'er yon clear fount her brow;
Long years, that leave their trace behind,
Long years, are present with her now.

Yet, once before she asked a sign
From that wild fountain's plaintive song;
And silvery, with the soft moonshine,
Those singing waters past along.

It was an hour of beauty, made
For the young heart's impassioned mood,
For love of its sweet self afraid,
For hope that colours solitude.

'Alas,' the maiden sighed, 'since first
I said, Oh fountain, read my doom;
What vainest fancies have I nurst,
Of which I am myself the tomb!

'The love was checked—the hope was vain,
I deemed that I could feel no more;
Why, false one, did we meet again,
To show thine influence was not o'er?

'I thought that I could never weep
Again, as I had wept for thee,
That love was buried cold and deep,
That pride and scorn kept watch by me.

'My early hopes, my early tears
Were now almost forgotten things,
And other cares, and other years
Had brought what all experience brings—

'Indifference, weariness, disdain,
That taught and ready smile which grows
A habit soon—as streams retain
The shape and light in which they froze.

'Again I met that faithless eye,
Again I heard that charmed tongue;
I felt they were my destiny,
I knew again the spell they flung.

'Ah! years have fled, since last his name
Was breathed amid the twilight dim;
It was to dream of him I came,
And now again I dream of him.

'But changed and cold, my soul has been
Too deeply wrung, too long unmoved,
Too hardened in life's troubled scene
To love as I could once have loved.

'Sweet fountain, once I asked thy waves
To whisper hope's enchanted spell;
Now I but ask thy haunted caves
To teach me how to say farewell.'

She leaned her head upon her hand,
She gazed upon that fountain lone
Which wandered by its wild-flower strand
With a low, mournful, ceaseless moan.

It soothed her with a sweet deceit
Of pity, murmured on the breeze;
Ah deep the grief, which seeks to cheat
Itself with fantasies like these.

The Record

He sleeps, his head upon his sword,
His soldier's cloak a shroud;
His church-yard is the open field,
Three times it has been plough'd:

The first time that the wheat sprung up
'Twas black as if with blood,
The meanest beggar turn'd away
From the unholy food.

The third year, and the grain grew fair,
As it was wont to wave;
None would have thought that golden corn
Was growing on the grave.

His lot was but a peasant's lot,
His name a peasant's name,
Not his the place of death that turns
Into a place of fame.

He fell as other thousands do,
Trampled down where they fall,
While on a single name is heap'd
The glory gain'd by all.

Yet even he whose common grave
Lies in the open fields,
Died not without a thought of all
The joy that glory yields.

That small white church in his own land,
The lime trees almost hide,
Bears on the walls the names of those
Who for their country died.

His name is written on those walls,
His mother read it there,
With pride, oh! no, there could not be
Pride in the widow's prayer.

And many a stranger who shall mark
That peasant roll of fame,
Will think on prouder ones, yet say
This was a hero's name.

The Sea-Shore

I should like to dwell where the deep blue sea
Rock'd to and fro as tranquilly,
As if it were willing the halcyon's nest

Should shelter through summer its beautiful guest.
When a plaining murmur like that of a song,
And a silvery line come the waves along:
Now bathing—now leaving the gentle shore,
Where shining sea-shells lay scattered o'er.

And children wandering along the strand,
With the eager eye and the busy hand,
Heaping the pebbles and green sea-weed,
Like treasures laid up for a time of need.
Or tempting the waves with their daring feet,
To launch, perhaps, some tiny fleet:
Mimicking those which bear afar
The wealth of trade—and the strength of war.

I should love, when the sun-set reddened the foam,
To watch the fisherman's boat come home,
With his well-filled net and glittering spoil:
Well has the noon-tide repaid its toil.
While the ships that lie in the distance away
Catch on their canvass the crimsoning ray;
Like fairy ships in the tales of old,
When the sails they spread were purple and gold.

Then the deep delight of the starry night,
With its shadowy depths and dreamy light:
When far away spreads the boundless sea,
As if it imaged infinity.
Let me hear the winds go singing by,
Lulling the waves with their melody:
While the moon like a mother watches their sleep,
And I ask no home but beside the deep.

The Soldier's Funeral

The muffled drum rolled on the air,
Warriors, with stately step, were there;
On every arm was the black crape bound,
Every carbine was turned to the ground;
Solemn, the sound of their measured tread,
As silent and slow, they followed the dead.

The riderless horse was led in the rear;
There were white plumes waving over the bier;
Helmet and sword were laid on the pall,
For, it was a soldier's funeral.

That soldier had stood on the battle plain,
Where every step was over the slain;
But the brand and the ball had passed him by,
And he came to his native land, to die.

'Twas hard to come to that native land,
And not clasp one familiar hand;
'Twas hard to be numbered amid the dead,
Before he could hear his welcome said.

But, 'twas something to see its cliffs once more,
And to lay his bones on his own loved shore;
To think, that the friends of his youth might weep,
O'er the green grass turf of the soldier's sleep.

The bugles ceased their wailing sound,
As the coffin was lowered into the ground;
A volley was fired, a blessing said,
One moment's pause, and they left the dead.

I saw a poor and aged man -
His step was feeble, his cheek was wan;
He knelt him down on the new-raised mound,
His face was bowed on the cold damp ground;
He raised his head, his tears were done -
The father had prayed o'er his only son.

Change

And this is what is left of youth! . . .
There were two boys, who were bred up together,
Shared the same bed, and fed at the same board;
Each tried the other's sport, from their first chase,
Young hunters of the butterfly and bee,
To when they followed the fleet hare, and tried
The swiftness of the bird. They lay beside
The silver trout stream, watching as the sun
Played on the bubbles: shared each in the store
Of either's garden: and together read
Of him, the master of the desert isle,
Till a low hut, a gun, and a canoe,
Bounded their wishes. Or if ever came
A thought of future days, 'twas but to say
That they would share each other's lot, and do
Wonders, no doubt. But this was vain: they parted
With promises of long remembrance, words
Whose kindness was the heart's, and those warm tears,
Hidden like shame by the young eyes which shed them,
But which are thought upon in after-years
As what we would give worlds to shed once more.

They met again, — but different from themselves,
At least what each remembered of themselves:
The one proud as a soldier of his rank,
And of his many battles: and the other

Proud of his Indian wealth, and of the skill
And toil which gathered it; each with a brow
And heart alike darkened by years and care.
They met with cold words, and yet colder looks:
Each was changed in himself, and yet each thought
The other only changed, himself the same.
And coldness bred dislike, and rivalry
Came like the pestilence o'er some sweet thoughts
That lingered yet, healthy and beautiful,
Amid dark and unkindly ones. And they,
Whose boyhood had not known one jarring word,
Were strangers in their age: if their eyes met,
'Twas but to look contempt, and when they spoke,
Their speech was wormwood! . . .
. . . And this, this is life!

The Song. Extract from The Zenana
'My lonely lute, how can I ask
For music from thy silent strings?
It is too sorrowful a task,
When only swept by memory's wings:
Yet waken from thy charmed sleep,
Although I wake thee but to weep.

'Yet once I had a thousand songs,
As now I have but only one.
Ah, love, whate'er to thee belongs.
With all life's other links, has done;
And I can breathe no other words
Than thou hast left upon the chords.

'They say Camdeo's place of rest,
When floating down the Ganges' tide,
Is in the languid lotus breast,
Amid whose sweets he loves to hide.
Oh, false and cruel, though divine,
What dost thou in so fair a shrine?

'And such the hearts that thou dost choose,
As pure, as fair, to shelter thee;
Alas! they know not what they lose
Who chance thy dwelling-place to be.
For, never more in happy dream
Will they float down life's sunny stream.

'My gentle lute, repeat one name,
The very soul of love, and thine:
No; sleep in silence, let me frame
Some other love to image mine;

Steal sadness from another's tone,
I dare not trust me with my own.

'Thy chords will win their mournful way,
All treasured thoughts to them belong;
For things it were so hard to say
Are murmured easily in song—
It is for music to impart
The secrets of the burthened heart.

'Go, taught by misery and love,
And thou hast spells for every ear:
But the sweet skill each pulse to move,
Alas! hath bought its knowledge dear—
Bought by the wretchedness of years,
A whole life dedicate to tears.'

The voice has ceased, the chords are mute,
The singer droops upon her lute;

But, oh, the fulness of each tone
Straight to Nadira's heart hath gone—
As if that mournful song revealed
Depths in that heart till then concealed,
A world of melancholy thought,
Then only into being brought;
Those tender mysteries of the soul,
Like words on an enchanted scroll,
Whose mystic meaning but appears
When washed and understood by tears.
She gazed upon the singer's face;
Deeply that young brow wore the trace
Of years that leave their stamp behind:
The wearied hope—the fever'd mind—
The heart which on itself hath turned,
Worn out with feelings—slighted—spurned—
Till scarce one throb remained to show
What warm emotions slept below,

Never to be renewed again,
And known but by remembered pain.
Her cheek was pale—impassioned pale—
Like ashes white with former fire,
Passion which might no more prevail,
The rose had been its own sweet pyre.
You gazed upon the large black eyes,
And felt what unshed tears were there;
Deep, gloomy, wild, like midnight skies,
When storms are heavy on the air—
And on the small red lip sat scorn,
Writhing from what the past had borne.

But far too proud to sigh—the will,
Though crushed, subdued, was haughty still;
Last refuge of the spirit's pain,
Which finds endurance in disdain.

Others wore blossoms in their hair,
And golden bangles round the arm.
She took no pride in being fair,
The gay delight of youth to charm;
The softer wish of love to please,
What had she now to do with these?
She knew herself a bartered slave,
Whose only refuge was the grave.
Unsoftened now by those sweet notes,
Which half subdued the grief they told,
Her long black hair neglected floats
O'er that wan face, like marble cold;
And carelessly her listless hand
Wandered above her lute's command
But silently—or just a tone
Woke into music, and was gone.

Children
A word will fill the little heart
With pleasure and with pride;
It is a harsh, a cruel thing,
That such can be denied.

And yet how many weary hours
Those joyous creatures know;
How much of sorrow and restraint
They to their elders owe!

How much they suffer from our faults!
How much from our mistakes!
How often, too, mistaken zeal
An infant's misery makes!

We overrule and overteach,
We curb and we confine,
And put the heart to school too soon,
To learn our narrow line.

No: only taught by love to love,
Seems childhood's natural task;
Affection, gentleness, and hope,
Are all its brief years ask.

Long Years Have Past Since Last I Stood

Long years have past since last I stood
Alone amid this mountain scene,
Unlike the future which I dreamed,
How like my future it has been!
A cold grey sky o'erhung with clouds,
With showers in every passing shade,
How like the moral atmosphere
Whose gloom my horoscope has made!

I thought if yet my weary feet
Could rove my native hills again,
A world of feeling would revive,
Sweet feelings wasted, worn in vain.
My early hopes, my early joys,
I dreamed those valleys would restore;
I asked for childhood to return,
For childhood, which returns no more.

Surely the scene itself is changed!
There did not always rest as now
That shadow in the valley's depth,
That gloom upon the mountain-brow.
Wild flowers within the chasms dwelt
Like treasures in stone fairy hold,
And morning o'er the mountains shed
Her kindling world of vapoury gold.

Another season of the year
Is now upon the earth and me;
Another spring will light these hills—
No other spring mine own may be:
I must retune my unstrung harp,
I must awake the sleeping tomb,
I must recall the loved and lost,
Ere spring again for me could bloom.

I've wandered, but it was in vain,
In many a far and foreign clime,
Absence is not forgetfulness,
And distance cannot vanquish time.
One face was ever in my sight,
One voice was ever on my ear,
From all earth's loveliness I turned
To wish, Ah that the dead were here!

Oh! weary wandering to no home,
Oh! weary wandering alone,
I turned to childhood's once glad scenes
And found life's last illusion flown.
Ah! those who left their childhood's scenes
For after-years of toil and pain,

Who but bring back the breaking heart
Should never seek those scenes again.

Secrets

Life has dark secrets; and the hearts are few
That treasure not some sorrow from the world
A sorrow silent, gloomy, and unknown,
Yet colouring the future from the past.
We see the eye subdued, the practised smile,
The word well weighed before it pass the lip,
And know not of the misery within:
Yet there it works incessantly, and fears
The time to come; for time is terrible,
Avenging, and betraying.

The Country Retreat

Oh lone and lovely solitude,
Washed by the sounding sea;
Nature was in a poet's mood,
When she created thee.

How pleasant in the hour of noon
To wander through the shade;
The soft and golden shade which
June Flings o'er thy inland glade:

The wild rose like a wreath above,
The ash-tree's fairy keys,
The aspen trembling, as if love
Were whispered by the breeze;

These, or the beech's darker bough,
For canopy o'er head,
While moss and fragile flowers below
An elfin pillow spread.

Here one might dream the hours away,
As if the world had not
Or grief, or care, or disarray,
To darken human lot.

Yet 'tis not here that I would dwell,
Though fair the place may be,
The summer's favourite citadel:—
A busier scene for me!

I love to see the human face
Reflect the human mind,
To watch in every crowded place

Their opposites combined.

There's more for thought in one brief hour
In yonder busy street,
Than all that ever leaf or flower
Taught in their green retreat.
Industry, intellect, and skill
Appear in all their pride,
The glorious force of human will
Triumphs on every side.

Yet touched with meekness, for on all
Is set the sign and seal
Of sorrow, suffering, and thrall,
Which none but own and feel;

The hearse that passes with its dead,
The homeless beggar's prayer,
Speak words of warning, and of dread,
To every passer there.

Aye beautiful the dreaming brought
By valleys and green fields;
But deeper feeling, higher thought,
Is what the city yields.

The Funeral
Mark you not yon sad procession;
'Mid the ruin'd abbey's gloom,
Hastening to the worm's possession,
To the dark and silent tomb!

See the velvet pall hangs over
Poor mortality's remains;
We should shudder to discover
What that coffin's space contains.

Death itself is lovely—wearing
But the colder shape of sleep;
Or the solemn statue bearing
Beauty that forbids to weep.

But decay—the pulses tremble
When its livid signs appear;
When the once-loved lips resemble
All we loathe, and all we fear.

Is it not a ghastly ending
For the body's godlike form,
Thus to the damp earth descending,

Food and triumph to the worm?

Better far the red pile blazing
With the spicy Indian wood,
Incense unto heaven raising
From the sandal oil's sweet flood.

In the bright pyre's kindling flashes,
Let my yielded soul ascend;
Fling to the wild winds my ashes
'Till with mother-earth they blend.

Not so,—let the pale urn keep them;
Touch'd with spices, oil, and wine;
Let there be some one to weep them;
Wilt thou keep that urn? Love mine!

A Legend Of Tintagel Castle

Alone in the forest, Sir Lancelot rode
O'er the neck of his courser the reins lightly flowed
And beside hung his helmet, for bare was his brow
To meet the soft breeze that was fanning him now.

And 'the flowers of the forest' were many and sweet,
Which, crushed at each step by his proud courser's feet,
Gave forth all their fragrance, while thick over-head
The boughs of the oak and the elm-tree were spread.

The wind stirred its branches, as if its low suit
Were urged, like a lover who wakens the lute,
And through the dark foliage came sparkling and bright
Like rain from the green leaves, in small gems of light.

There was stillness, not silence, for dancing along,
A brook went its way like a child with a song;
Now hidden, where rushes and water-flags grow;
Now clear, while white pebbles were glistening below.

Lo, bright as a vision, and fair as a dream,
The face of a maiden is seen in the stream;
With her hair like a mantle of gold to her knee,
Stands a lady as lovely as lady can be.

Short speech tells a love-tale;—the bard's sweetest words
Are poor, beside those which each memory hoards;
Sound of some gentle whisper, the haunting and low,
Such as love may have murmured—ah, long, long ago.

She led him away to an odorous cave,
Where the emerald spars shone like stars in the wave,

And the green moss and violets crowded beneath,
And the ash at the entrance hung down like a wreath.

They might have been happy, if love could but learn
A lesson from some flowers, and like their leaves turn
Round their own inward world, their own lone fragrant nest,
Content with its sweetness, content with its rest.

But the sound of the trumpet was heard from afar,
And Sir Lancelot rode forth again to the war;
And the wood-nymph was left as aye woman will be,
Who trusts her whole being, oh, false love, to thee.

For months, every sunbeam that brightened the gloom,
She deemed was the waving of Lancelot's plume;
She knew not of the proud and the beautiful queen,
Whose image was treasured as hers once had been.

There was many a fair dame, and many a knight,
Made the banks of the river like fairy-land bright;
And among those whose shadow was cast on the tide,
Was Lancelot kneeling at Genevra's side.

With purple sails heavily drooping around
The mast, and the prow, with the vale lily bound;
And towed by two swans, a small vessel drew near
But high on the deck was a pall-covered bier.

They oared with their white wings, the bark thro' the flood,
Till arrived at the bank where Sir Lancelot stood:
A wind swept the river, and flung back the pall,
And there lay a lady, the fairest of all.

But pale as a statue, like sunshine on snow,
The bright hair seemed mocking the cold face below:
Sweet truants, the blush and the smile both are fled—
Sir Lancelot weeps as he kneels by the dead.

And these are love's records; a vow and a dream,
And the sweet shadow passes away from life's stream:
Too late we awake to regret—but what tears
Can bring back the waste to our hearts and our years?

Cafes In Damascus
Languidly the night-wind bloweth
From the gardens round,
Where the clear Barrada floweth
With a lulling sound.

Not the lute-note's sweet shiver

Can such music find,
As is on a wandering river,
On a wandering wind.

There the Moslem leaneth, dreaming
O'er the inward world,
While around the fragrant steaming
Of the smoke is curled.

Rising from the coffee berry,
Dark grape of the South;
Or the pipe of polished cherry,
With its amber mouth.

Cooled by passing through the water,
Gurgling as it flows—
Scented by the Summer's daughter,
June's impassioned rose.

By that rose's spirit haunted
Are the dreams that rise,
Of far lands, and lives enchanted,
And of deep black eyes.

Thus with some sweet dream's assistance,
Float they down life's stream;
Would to heaven our whole existence
Could be such a dream!

Furness Abbey

I wish for the days of the olden time,
When the hours were told by the abbey chime,
When the glorious stars looked down through the midnigh dim,
Like approving saints on the choir's sweet hymn:
I think of the days we are living now,
And I sigh for those of the veil and the vow.

I would be content alone to dwell
Where the ivy shut out the sun from my cell,
With the death's-head at my side, and the missal on my knee,
Praying to that heaven which was opening to me:
Fevered and vain are the days I lead now,
And I sigh for those of the veil and the vow.

Silken broidery no more would I wear,
Nor golden combs in my golden hair;
I wore them but for one, and in vain they were worn;
My robe should be of serge, my crown of the thorn:
'Tis a cold false world we dwell in now,
And I sigh for the days of the veil and the vow.

I would that the cloister's quiet were mine;
In the silent depths of some holy shrine.

I would tell my blessed beads, and would weep away
From my inmost soul every stain of clay:
My heart's young hopes they have left me now,
And I sigh for the days of the veil and the vow.

Girl At Her Devotions

She was just risen from her bended knee,
But yet peace seem'd not with her piety;
For there was paleness upon her young cheek,
And thoughts upon the lips which never speak,
But wring the heart that at the last they break.
Alas! how much of misery may be read
In that wan forehead, and that bow'd down head:
Her eye is on a picture, woe that ever
Love should thus struggle with a vain endeavour
Against itself: it is a common tale,
And ever will be while earth soils prevail
Over earth's happiness; it tells she strove
With silent, secret, unrequited love.

It matters not its history; love has wings
Like lightining , swift and fatal, and it springs
Like a wild flower where it is least expected,
Existing whether cherish'd or rejected;
Living with only but to be content,
Hopeless, for love is its own element,
Requiring nothing so that it may be
The martyr of its fond fidelity.
A mystery art thou, thou mighty one!
We speak thy name in beauty, yet we shun
To own thee, Love, a guest; the poet's songs
Are sweetest when their voice to thee belongs,
And hope, sweet opiate, tenderness, delight,
Are terms which are thy own peculiar right;
Yet all deny their master, who will own
His breast thy footstool, and his heart thy throne?

'Tis strange to think if we could fling aside
The masque and mantle that love wears from pride,
How much would be, we now so little guess,
Deep in each heart's undream'd, unsought recess.
The careless smile, like a gay banner borne,
The laugh of merriment, the lip of scorn,
And for a cloak what is there that can be
So difficult to pierce as gaiety?
Too dazzling to be scann'd, the haughty brow

Seems to hide something it would not avow;
But rainbow words, light laugh, and thoughtless jest,
These are the bars, the curtain to the breast,
That shuns a scrutiny: and she, whose form
Now bends in grief beneath the bosom's storm,
Has hidden well her wound, now none are nigh
To mock with curious or with careless eye,
(For love seeks sympathy, a chilling yes,
Strikes at the root of its best happiness,
And mockery is worm-wood), she may dwell
On feelings which that picture may not tell.

Hannibal's Oath

And the night was dark and calm,
There was not a breath of air,
The leaves of the grove were still,
As the presence of death were there;

Only a moaning sound
Came from the distant sea,
It was as if, like life,
It had no tranquillity.

A warrior and a child
Pass'd through the sacred wood,
Which, like a mystery,
Around the temple stood.

The warrior's brow was worn
With the weight of casque and plume,
And sun-burnt was his cheek,
And his eye and brow were gloom.

The child was young and fair,
But the forehead large and high,
And the dark eyes' flashing light
Seem'd to feel their destiny.

They enter'd in the temple,
And stood before the shrine,
It stream'd with the victim's blood,
With incense and with wine.

The ground rock'd beneath their feet,
The thunder shook the dome,
But the boy stood firm, and swore
Eternal hate to Rome.

There's a page in history
O'er which tears of blood were wept,

And that page is the record
How that oath of hate was kept.

The African Prince

It was a king in Africa,
He had an only son;
And none of Europe's crowned kings
Could have a dearer one.

With good cane arrows five feet long,
And with a shining bow,
When but a boy, to the palm woods
Would that young hunter go.

And home he brought white ivory,
And many a spotted hide:
When leopards fierce and beautiful
Beneath his arrows died.

Around his arms, around his brow,
A shining bar was rolled;
It was to mark his royal blood,
He wore that bar of gold.

And often at his father's feet,
The evening he would pass;
When, weary of the hunt, he lay
Upon the scented grass.

Alas! it was an evil day,
When such a thing could be:
When strangers, pale and terrible,
Came o'er the distant sea.

They found the young prince mid the woods,
The palm woods deep and dark:
That day his lion-hunt was done,
They bore him to their bark.

They bound him in a narrow hold,
With others of his kind;
For weeks did that accursed ship
Sail on before the wind.
Now shame upon the cruel wind,
And on the cruel sea,
That did not with some mighty storm,
Set those poor captives free:

Or, shame to those weak thoughts, so fain
To have their wilful way:

God knoweth what is best for all—
The winds and seas obey.

At length a lovely island rose
From out the ocean wave;
They took him to the market-place,
And sold him for a slave.

Some built them homes, and in the shade
Of flowered and fragrant trees,
They half forgot the palm-hid huts
They left far o'er the seas.

But he was born of nobler blood,
And was of nobler kind;
And even unto death, his heart
For its own kindred pined.

There came to him a seraph child
With eyes of gentlest blue:
If there are angels in high heaven,
Earth has its angels too.

She cheered him with her holy words,
She soothed him with her tears;
And pityingly she spoke with him
Of home and early years.

And when his heart was all subdued
By kindness into love,
She taught him from this weary earth
To look in faith above.

She told him how the Saviour died
For man upon the tree;
'He suffered,' said the holy child,
'For you as well as me.'

Sorrow and death have need of faith—
The African believed;
As rain falls fertile on the earth
Those words his soul received.

He died in hope as only those
Who die in Christ depart—
One blessed name within his lips,
One hope within his heart.

The Crusader
He is come from the land of the sword and shrine,

From the sainted battles of Palestine;
The snow plumes wave o'er his victor crest,
Like a glory, the red cross hangs at his breast;
His courser is black, as black can be,
Save the brow star, white as the foam of the sea,
And he wears a scarf of broidery rare,
The last love gift of his lady fair;
It bore for device a cross and a dove,
And the words - 'I am vowed to my God and my love.'

He comes not back the same that he went;
For his sword has been tried, and his strength has been spent,
His golden hair has a deeper brown,
And his brow has caught a darker frown;
And his lip has lost its youthful red,
And the shade of the South o'er his cheek is spread,
But stately his step, and his bearing high,
And wild the light of his fiery eye;
And proud in the lists were the maiden bright,
Who might claim the Knight of the Cross for her knight.

He rides for the home he had pined to see,
In the court, in the camp, in captivity!
He reached the castle - his own step was all
That echoed within the deserted hall;
He stood on the roof of the ancient tower;
And, for banner, there waved one pale wall flower,
And, for sound of the trumpet and peal of the horn,
Came the scream of the owl, on the night wind borne.
The turrets were falling, the vassals were flown,
And the bat ruled the halls, he had called his own;
His heart throbbed high - Oh! never again
Might he soothe with sweet thoughts his spirit's pain;
He never might think of his boyish years,
Till his eyes grew dim with those sweet warm tears,
Which hope and memory shed when they meet -
The grave of his kindred was at his feet -
He stood alone, the last of his race,
With the cold wide world for his dwelling place;
The home of his fathers gone to decay,
All but their memory had passed away -
No one to welcome, no one to share
The laurel, he no more was proud to wear.
He came, in the pride of his war-success,
But to weep over very desolateness.

They pointed him to a barren plain,
Where his father, his brothers, his kinsmen were slain;
They shewed him the lowly grave, where slept
The maiden, whose scarf he so truly had kept;
But they could not shew him one living thing,

To which his withered heart could cling -

Amid the warriors of Palestine
Is one, the first in the battle line.
It is not for glory he seeks the field,
For a blasted tree is upon his shield,
And the motto it bears is, 'I fight for a grave.'
He found it - That warrior has died with the brave.

The Minister

Dim thro' the sculptured aisles the sunbeam falls
More like a dream
Of some imagined beam,
Than actual daylight over mortal walls.

A strain of music like the rushing wind,
But deep and sweet
As when the waters meet
In one mysterious harmony combined.

So swells the mighty organ, rich and full,
As if it were the soul
Which raised the glorious whole
Of that fair building, vast and wonderful.

Doth not the spirit feel its influence,
All vain and feverish care,
All thoughts that worldly are,
Strife, tumult, mirth, and fear are vanished hence.

The world is put aside, within the heart
Those hopes arise
Thrice sacred mysteries,
In which our earthly nature has no part.

Oh, Christian Fane, the soul expands in thee,
Thine altar and thy tomb
Speak of the hope and doom
Which leads and cheers man to eternity.

Sir Walter Scott

Dead!—it was like a thunderbolt
To hear that he was dead;
Though for long weeks the words of fear
Came from his dying bed;
Yet hope denied, and would deny—
We did not think that he could die.

The poet has a glorious hold
Upon the human heart,
Yet glory is from sympathy
A light alone—apart;
But there was something in thy name,
Which touched us with a dearer claim

The earnest feeling borne to thee
Was like a household tie,
A sunshine on our common life,
And from our daily sky.
Thy works are those familiar things
From which so much of memory springs.

We talked of them beside the hearth,
Till every story blends
With some remembered intercourse
Of near and dearest friends,
Friends that in early youth were ours.
Connected with life's happiest hours.

How well I can recall the time
When first I turned thy page,
The green boughs closed above my head
A natural hermitage;
And sang a little brook along,
As if it heard and caught thy song.

I peopled all the walks and shades
With images of thine;
The lime-tree was a lady's bower,
The yew-tree was a shrine:
Almost I deemed each sunbeam shone
O'er banner, spear, and morion.

Now, not one single trace is left
Of that sequestered nook;
The very course is turned aside
Of that melodious brook:
Not so the memories can depart,
Then garner'd in my inmost heart.
The past was his—his generous song
Went back to other days,
With filial feeling, which still sees
Something to love and praise,
And closer drew the ties which bind
Man with his country and his kind.

It rang throughout his native land,
A bold and stirring song,
As the merle's hymn at matin sweet,

And as the trumpet strong:
A touch there was of each degree,
Half minstrel and half knight was he.

How many a lonely mountain glade
Lives in his verse anew,
Linked with associate sympathy,
The tender and the true;
For nature has fresh beauty brought,
When animate with life from thought.

'Tis not the valley nor the hill,
Tho' beautiful they be,
That can suffice the heart, till touched
As they were touched by thee;
Thou who didst glorify the whole,
By pouring forth the poet's soul.

Who now could stand upon the banks
Of thine own 'silver Tweed?'
Nor deem they heard thy 'warrior's horn,'
Or heard thy 'shepherd's reed?'
Immutable as Nature's claim,
The ground is hallowed by thy name.

I cannot bear to see the shelf
Where ranged thy volumes stand,
And think that mute is now thy lip,
And cold is now thy hand;
That, hadst thou been more common clay,
So soon thou hadst not passed sway,

For thou didst die before thy time,
The tenement o'erwrought,
The heart consumed by its desire,
The body worn by thought;
Thyself the victim of thy shrine,
A glorious sacrifice was thine.

Alas, it is too soon for this—
The future for thy fame;
But now we mourn as if we mourned
A father's cherished claim.
Ah! time may bid the laurel wave—
We can but weep above thy grave.

The Power of Words

'Tis a strange mystery, the power of words!
Life is in them, and death. A word can send
The crimson colour hurrying to the cheek.

Hurrying with many meanings; or can turn
The current cold and deadly to the heart.
Anger and fear are in them; grief and joy
Are on their sound; yet slight, impalpable:
A word is but a breath of passing air.

The Record
He sleeps, his head upon his sword,
His soldier's cloak a shroud;
His church-yard is the open field,
Three times it has been plough'd:

The first time that the wheat sprung up
'Twas black as if with blood,
The meanest beggar turn'd away
From the unholy food.

The third year, and the grain grew fair,
As it was wont to wave;
None would have thought that golden corn
Was growing on the grave.

His lot was but a peasant's lot,
His name a peasant's name,
Not his the place of death that turns
Into a place of fame.

He fell as other thousands do,
Trampled down where they fall,
While on a single name is heap'd
The glory gain'd by all.

Yet even he whose common grave
Lies in the open fields,
Died not without a thought of all
The joy that glory yields.

That small white church in his own land,
The lime trees almost hide,
Bears on the walls the names of those
Who for their country died.

His name is written on those walls,
His mother read it there,
With pride, oh! no, there could not be
Pride in the widow's prayer.

And many a stranger who shall mark
That peasant roll of fame,
Will think on prouder ones, yet say

This was a hero's name.

The Reply Of The Fountain

How deep within each human heart,
A thousand treasured feelings lie;
Things precious, delicate, apart,
Too sensitive for human eye.

Our purest feelings, and our best,
Yet shrinking from the common view;
Rarely except in song exprest,
And yet how tender, and how true!

They wake, and know their power, when eve
Flings on the west its transient glow;
Yet long dark shadows dimly weave
A gloom round some green path below.

Who dreams not then—the young dream on—
Life traced at hope's delicious will;
And those whose youth of heart is gone,
Perhaps have visions dearer still.

They rise, too, when expected least,
When gay yourself, amid the gay,
The heart from revelry hath ceased
To muse o'er hours long past away.

And who can think upon the past
And not weep o'er it as a grave?
How many leaves life's wreath has cast!
What lights have sunk beneath the wave!

But most these deep emotions rise
When, drooping o'er our thoughts alone,
Our former dearest sympathies
Come back, and claim us for their own.

Such mood is on the maiden's mind
Who bends o'er yon clear fount her brow;
Long years, that leave their trace behind,
Long years, are present with her now.

Yet, once before she asked a sign
From that wild fountain's plaintive song;
And silvery, with the soft moonshine,
Those singing waters past along.

It was an hour of beauty, made
For the young heart's impassioned mood,

For love of its sweet self afraid,
For hope that colours solitude.

'Alas,' the maiden sighed, 'since first
I said, Oh fountain, read my doom;
What vainest fancies have I nurst,
Of which I am myself the tomb!

'The love was checked—the hope was vain,
I deemed that I could feel no more;
Why, false one, did we meet again,
To show thine influence was not o'er?

'I thought that I could never weep
Again, as I had wept for thee,
That love was buried cold and deep,
That pride and scorn kept watch by me.

'My early hopes, my early tears
Were now almost forgotten things,
And other cares, and other years
Had brought what all experience brings—

'Indifference, weariness, disdain,
That taught and ready smile which grows
A habit soon—as streams retain
The shape and light in which they froze.

'Again I met that faithless eye,
Again I heard that charmed tongue;
I felt they were my destiny,
I knew again the spell they flung.

'Ah! years have fled, since last his name
Was breathed amid the twilight dim;
It was to dream of him I came,
And now again I dream of him.

'But changed and cold, my soul has been
Too deeply wrung, too long unmoved,
Too hardened in life's troubled scene
To love as I could once have loved.

'Sweet fountain, once I asked thy waves
To whisper hope's enchanted spell;
Now I but ask thy haunted caves
To teach me how to say farewell.'

She leaned her head upon her hand,
She gazed upon that fountain lone
Which wandered by its wild-flower strand

With a low, mournful, ceaseless moan.

It soothed her with a sweet deceit
Of pity, murmured on the breeze;
Ah deep the grief, which seeks to cheat
Itself with fantasies like these.

The Ruined Cottage

None will dwell in that cottage; for, they say
Oppression reft it from an honest man,
And that a curse clings to it. Hence the vine
Trails its green weight of leaves upon the ground;
Hence weeds are in the garden; hence the hedge,
Once sweet with honey suckle, is half-dead;
And hence the gray moss on the apple tree.
One once dwelt there, who, in his youth,
Had been a soldier; and, when many days
Had passed, he sought his native village,
And sat down, to end his days in peace.
He had one child, a little laughing thing,
Whose dark eyes, he said, were like her mother's,
She had left buried in a strange land.
And time went on in comfort and content;
And that fair girl had grown far taller
Than the red-rose tree, her father planted
On her first English birth-day. He had trained it
Against an ash, till it became his pride,
It was so rich in blossom and in beauty.
It was called the tree of Isabel. 'Twas an appeal
To all the finer feelings of the heart
To mark their quiet happiness; their home,
In truth, the house of love; and, more than all,
To see them on the Sabbath, when they came,
Among the first, to church. And Isabel,
With her bright colour and her clear blue eyes,
Bowed down so meekly in the house of prayer;
And, in the hymn, her sweet voice audible.
Her father looked so fond of her, and then,
From her looked up so thankfully to heaven.
Then their small cottage was so very neat,
Their garden filled with fruits and flowers and herbs;
And in the winter there was no fireside
So cheerful as their own.
But other days
And other fortunes came - and evil power;
They bore against it cheerfully, and hoped
For better times; but ruin came at last,
And the old soldier left his dear home,
And left it for a prison. 'Twas in June,
One of June's brightest days; the bee, the bird,

The butterfly, were on their lightest wings;
The fruits had their first tinge of summer light;
The sunny sky, the very leaves seemed glad;
But the old man looked back upon his cottage,
And wept aloud. They hurried him away,
And the dear child, that would not leave his side!
They led him from the sight of the blue heaven
And the green grass, into a low dark cell,
The windows shutting out the blessed sun
With iron grating; and, for the first time,
He threw him on the bed, and could not hear
His Isabel's good night.
But the next morn
She was the earliest at the prison gate,
The last on whom it closed, and her sweet voice
And sweeter smile made him forget to pine.
She brought him every morning fresh wild flowers,
But every morning he could mark her cheek
Grow paler and more pale, and her low tones
Get fainter and more faint; and a cold dew
Was on the hand he held. One day he saw
The sun shine through the grating of his cell,
Yet Isabel came not. At every sound
His heart-beat took away his breath;
Yet still she came not near him. One sad day
He marked the dull street, through the iron bars,
That shut him from the world. At length,
He saw a coffin carried carelessly along;
And he grew desperate. He forced the bars;
And he stood on the street, free and alone.
He had no aim, no wish for liberty;
He only felt one want - to see the corpse,
That had no mourners. When they set it down,
Ere it was lowered into the new-dug grave,
A rush of passion came upon his soul;
He tore off the lid, and saw the face
Of Isabel, and knew he had no child.
He lay down by the coffin quietly -
His heart was broken!

The Soldier's Grave
There's a white stone placed upon yonder tomb,
Beneath is a soldier lying -
The death-wound came, amid sword and plume,
When banner and ball were flying.

Yet now he sleeps, the turf on his breast,
By wet wild flowers surrounded;
The church shadow falls o'er the place of his rest,
Where the steps of his childhood bounded.

There were tears, that fell from manly eyes,
There was woman's gentle weeping,
And the wailing of age and infant cries,
O'er the grave, where he lies sleeping.

He had left his home in his spirit's pride,
With his father's sword and blessing;
He stood with the valiant, side by side,
His country's wrongs redressing.

He came again, in the light of his fame,
When the red campaign was over;
One heart, that, in secret, had kept his name,
Was claimed by the soldier lover.

But the cloud of strife came upon the sky;-
He left his sweet home for battle;
Left his young child's lisp for the loud war-cry,
And the cannon's long death-rattle.

He came again - but an altered man:
The path of the grave was before him,
And the smile, that he wore, was cold and wan,
For the shadow of death hung o'er him.

He spoke of victory - spoke of cheer:-
These are the words, that are vainly spoken
To the childless mother, or orphan's ear,
Or the widow, whose heart is broken.

A helmet and sword are engraved on the stone,
Half hidden by yonder willow;
There he sleeps, whose death in battle was won,
But he died on his own home pillow.

The Shepherd Boy
Like some vision olden
Of far other time,
When the age was golden,
In the young world's prime
Is thy soft pipe ringing,
O lonely shepherd boy,
What song art thou singing,
In thy youth and joy?

Or art thou complaining
Of thy lowly lot,
And thine own disdaining
Dost ask what thou hast not?

Of the future dreaming,
Weary of the past,
For the present scheming,
All but what thou hast.

No, thou art delighting
In thy summer home;
Where the flowers inviting
Tempt the bee to roam;
Where the cowslip bending,
With its golden bells,
Of each glad hour's ending
With a sweet chime tells.

All wild creatures love him
When he is alone,
Every bird above him
Sings its softest tone.
Thankful to high Heaven,
Humble in thy joy,
Much to thee is given,
Lowly shepherd boy.

Thoughts Of Christmas-Day In India

It is Christmas, and the sunshine
Lies golden on the fields,
And flowers of white and purple
Yonder fragrant creeper yields.

Like the plumes of some bold warrior,
The cocoa-tree on high,
Lifts aloft its feathery branches,
Amid the deep blue sky.

From yonder shadowy peepul,
The pale fair lilac dove,
Like music from a temple,
Sings a song of grief and love.

The earth is bright with blossoms,
And a thousand jewelled wings,
Mid the green boughs of the tamarind
A sudden sunshine flings.

For the East, is earth's first-born,
And hath a glorious dower,
As Nature there had lavished
Her beauty and her power.

And yet I pine for England,

For my own—my distant home:
My heart is in that island,
Where'er my steps may roam.

It is merry there at Christmas—
We have no Christmas here;
'Tis a weary thing, a summer
That lasts throughout the year

I remember how the banners
Hung round our ancient hall,
Bound with wreaths of shining holly,
Brave winter's coronal.

And above each rusty helmet
Waved a new and cheering plume,
A branch of crimson berries,
And the latest rose in bloom.

And the white and pearly misletoe
Hung half concealed o'er head,
I remember one sweet maiden,
Whose cheek it dyed with red.

The morning waked with carols,
A young and joyous band
Of small and rosy songsters,
Came tripping hand in hand.

And sang beneath our windows
Just as the round red sun
Began to melt the hoar-frost,
And the clear cold day begun.

And at night the aged harper
Played his old tunes o'er and o'er;
From sixteen up to sixty,
All were dancing on that floor.

Those were the days of childhood,
The buoyant and the bright;
When hope was life's sweet sovereign,
And the heart and step were light.

I shall come again—a stranger
To all that once I knew,
For the hurried steps of manhood
From life's flowers have dash'd the dew.

I yet may ask their welcome,
And return from whence I came;

But a change is wrought within me,
They will not seem the same

For my spirits are grown weary,
And my days of youth are o'er,
And the mirth of that glad season
Is what I can feel no more.

To Olinthus Gregory, On Hearing Of The Death Of His Eldest Son, Who Was Drowned As He Was Returning By Water To His Father's House At Woolrich
Is there a spot where Pity's foot,
Although unsandalled, fears to tread,
A silence where her voice is mute,
Where tears, and only tears, are shed?
It is the desolated home
Where Hope was yet a recent guest,
Where Hope again may never come,
Or come, and only speak of rest.

They gave my hand the pictured scroll,
And bade me only fancy there
A parent's agony of soul,
A parent's long and last despair;
The sunshine on the sudden wave,
Which closed above the youthful head,
Mocking the green and quiet grave,
Which waits the time-appointed dead.

I thought upon the lone fire-side,
Begirt with all familiar thought,
The future, where a father's pride
So much from present promise wrought:
The sweet anxiety of fears,
Anxious from love's excess alone,
The fond reliance upon years
More precious to us than our own:

All past—then weeping words there came
From out a still and darkened room,
They could not bear to name a name
Written so newly on the tomb.
They said he was so good and kind,
The voices sank, the eyes grew dim;
So much of love he left behind,
So much of life had died with him.

Ah, pity for the long beloved,
Ah, pity for the early dead;
The young, the promising, removed
Ere life a light or leaf had shed.

Nay, rather pity those whose doom
It is to wait and weep behind,
The father, who within the tomb
Sees all life held most dear enshrined.

She Sat Alone Beside Her Hearth

She sat alone beside her hearth—
For many nights alone;
She slept not on the pleasant couch
Where fragrant herbs were strewn.

At first she bound her raven hair
With feather and with shell;
But then she hoped; at length, like night,
Around her neck it fell.

They saw her wandering mid the woods,
Lone, with rite cheerless dawn,
And then they said, 'Can this be her
We called 'The Startled Fawn?' '

Her heart was in her large sad eyes,
Half sunshine and half shade;
And love, as love first springs to life,
Of everything afraid.

The red leaf far more heavily
Fell down to autumn earth,
Than her light feet, which seemed to move
To music and to mirth.

With the light feet of early youth,
What hopes and joys depart,
Ah! nothing like the heavy step
Betrays the heavy heart.

It is a usual history
That Indian girl could tell;
Fate sets apart one common doom
For all who love too well.

The proud—the shy—the sensitive,
Life has not many such;
They dearly buy their happiness,
By feeling it too much.

A stranger to her forest home,
That fair young stranger came;
They raised for him the funeral song—
For him the funeral flame.

Love sprang from pity,—and her arms
Around his arms she threw;
She told her father, 'If he dies,
Your daughter dieth too.'

For her sweet sake they set him free—
He lingered at her side;
And many a native song yet tells
Of that pale stranger's bride.

Two years have passed—how much two years
Have taken in their flight!
They've taken from the lip its smile,
And from the eye its light.

Poor child! she was a child in years—
So timid and so young;
With what a fond and earnest faith
To desperate hope she clung!

His eyes grew cold—his voice grew strange—
They only grew more dear.
She served him meekly, anxiously,
With love—half faith—half fear.

And can a fond and faithful heart
Be worthless in those eyes
For which it beats?—Ah! wo to those
Who such a heart despise.

Poor child! what lonely days she passed,
With nothing to recall
But bitter taunts, and careless words,
And looks more cold than all.

Alas! for love, that sits at home,
Forsaken, and yet fond;
The grief that sits beside the hearth—
Life has no grief beyond.

He left her, but she followed him—
She thought he could not bear,
When she had left her home for him,
To look on her despair.

Adown the strange and mighty stream
She took her lonely way;
The stars at night her pilots were,
As was the sun by day.

Yet mournfully—how mournfully!—
The Indian looked behind,
When the last sound of voice or step
Died on the midnight wind,

Yet still adown the gloomy stream
She plied her weary oar;
Her husband—he had left their home,
And it was home no more.

She found him—but she found in vain—
He spurned her from his side;
He said, her brow was all too dark,
For her to be his bride.

She grasped his hands,—her own were cold,—
And silent turned away,
As she had not a tear to shed,
And not a word to say.

And pale as death she reached her boat,
And guided it along;
With broken voice she strove to raise
A melancholy song.

None watched the lonely Indian girl,—
She passed unmarked of all,
Until they saw her slight canoe
Approach the mighty Fall!

Upright, within that slender boat
They saw the pale girl stand,
Her dark hair streaming far behind—
Upraised her desperate hand.

The air is filled with shriek and shout—
They call, but call in vain;
The boat amid the waters dash'd—
'Twas never seen again!

The Sultana's Remonstrance
It suits thee well to weep,
As thou lookest on the fair land,
Whose sceptre thou hast held
With less than woman's hand.

On yon bright city gaze,
With its white and marble halls,
The glory of its lofty towers,
The strength of its proud walls.

And look to yonder palace,
With its garden of the rose,
With its groves and silver fountains,
Fit for a king's repose.

There is weeping in that city,
And a cry of woe and shame,
There's a whisper of dishonour,
And that whisper is thy name.

And the stranger's feast is spread,
But it is no feast of thine;
In thine own halls accursed lips
Drain the forbidden wine.

And aged men are in the streets,
Who mourn their length of days,
And young knights stand with folded arms,
And eyes they dare not raise.

There is not one whose blood was not
As the waves of ocean free,
Their fathers died for thy fathers,
They would have died for thee.

Weep not, 'tis mine to weep,
That ever thou wert born,
Alas, that all a mother's love
Is lost in a queen's scorn!

Yet weep, thou less than woman, weep,
Those tears become thine eye,
It suits thee well to weep the land
For which thou daredst not die.*

The Fairy Queen Sleeping
She lay upon a bank, the favourite haunt
Of the spring wind in its first sunshine hour,
For the luxuriant strawberry blossoms spread
Like a snow-shower there, and violets
Bow'd down their purple vases of perfume
About her pillow, link'd in a gay band
Floated fantastic shapes, these were her guards,
Her lithe and rainbow elves.

We have been o'er land and sea,
Seeking lovely dreams for thee,
Where is there we have not been
Gathering gifts for our sweet queen?

We are come with sound and sight
Fit for fairy's sleep to-night,
First around thy couch shall sweep
Odours, such as roses weep
When the earliest spring rain
Calls them into life again;
Next upon thine ear shall float
Many a low and silver note,
Stolen from a dark-eyed maid
When her lover's serenade,
Rising as the stars grew dim,
Waken'd her from thoughts of him.
There shall steal o'er lip and cheek
Gales, but all too light to break
Thy soft rest, such gales as hide
All day orange-flowers inside,
Or that, while hot noontide, dwell
In the purple hyacinth bell;
And before thy sleeping eyes
Shall come glorious pageantries,
Palaces of gems and gold,
Such as dazzle to behold,
Gardens, in which every tree
Seems a world of bloom to be,
Fountains, whose clear waters show
The white pearls that lie below.
During slumber's magic reign
Other times shall live again;
First thou shalt be young and free
In thy days of liberty,
Then again be woo'd and won
By thy stately Oberon.
Or thou shalt descend to earth,
And see all of mortal birth.

No, that world's too full of care
For e'en dreams to linger there.
But, behold, the sun is set,
And the diamond coronet
Of the young moon is on high
Waiting for our revelry;
And the dew is on the flower,
And the stars proclaim our hour;
Long enough thy rest has been,
Wake, Titania , wake our queen!

The Hindoo Girl's Song
Float on—float on—my haunted bark,
Above the midnight tide;
Bear softly o'er the waters dark

The hopes that with thee glide.

Float on—float on—thy freight is flowers,
And every flower reveals
The dreaming of my lonely hours,
The hope my spirit feels.

Float on—float on—thy shining lamp,
The light of love, is there;
If lost beneath the waters damp,
That love must then despair.

Float on—beneath the moonlight float
The sacred billows o'er:
Ah, some kind spirit guards my boat,
For it has gained the shore.

A Suttee

Gather her raven hair in one rich cluster,
Let the white champac light it, as a star
Gives to the dusky night a sudden lustre,
Shining afar.

Shed fragrant oils upon her fragrant bosom,
Until the breathing air around grows sweet;
Scatter the languid jasmine's yellow blossom
Beneath her feet.

Those small white feet are bare—too soft are they
To tread on aught but flowers; and there is roll'd
Round the slight ankle, meet for such display,
The band of gold.

Chains and bright stones are on her arms and neck;
What pleasant vanities are linked with them,
Of happy hours, which youth delights to deck
With gold and gem.

She comes! So comes the Moon, when she has found
A silvery path wherein thro' heaven to glide.
Fling the white veil—a summer cloud—around;
She is a bride!

And yet the crowd that gather at her side
Are pale, and every gazer holds his breath.
Eyes fill with tears unbidden, for the bride—
The bride of Death!

She gives away the garland from her hair,
She gives the gems that she will wear no more;

All the affections, whose love-signs they were,
Are gone before.

The red pile blazes—let the bride ascend,
And lay her head upon her husband's heart,
Now in a perfect unison to blend—
No more to part.

Alexander And Phillip
He stood by the river's side
A conqueror and a king,
None match'd his step of pride
Amid the armed ring.
And a heavy echo rose from the ground,
As a thousand warriors gather'd round.
And the morning march had been long,
And the noontide sun was high,
And weariness bow'd down the strong,
And heat closed every eye;
And the victor stood by the river's brim
Whose coolness seem'd but made for him.

The cypress spread their gloom
Like a cloak from the noontide beam,
He flung back his dusty plume,
And plunged in the silver stream;
He plunged like the young steed, fierce and wild,
He was borne away like the feeble child.

They took the king to his tent
From the river's fatal banks,
A cry of terror went
Like a storm through the Grecian ranks:
Was this the fruit of their glories won,
Was this the death for Ammon's son?

Many a leech heard the call,
But each one shrank away;
For heavy upon all
Was the weight of fear that day:
When a thought of treason, a word of death,
Was in each eye, and on each breath.

But one with the royal youth
Had been from his earliest hour,
And he knew that his heart was truth,
And he knew that his hand was power;
He gave what hope his skill might give,
And bade him trust to his faith and live.

Alexander took the cup,
And from beneath his head a scroll,
He drank the liquor up,
And bade Phillip read the roll;
And Phillip look'd on the page, where shame,
Treason, and poison were named with his name.

An angry flush rose on his brow,
And anger darken'd his eye,
What I have done I would do again now!
If you trust my fidelity.
The king watch'd his face, he felt he might dare
Trust the faith that was written there.

Next day the conqueror rose
From a greater conqueror free;
And again he stood amid those
Who had died his death to see:
He stood there proud of the lesson he gave
That faith and trust were made for the brave.

Fountain's Abbey

Never more, when the day is o'er,
Will the lonely vespers sound;
No bells are ringing—no monks are singing,
When the moonlight falls around.

A few pale flowers, which in other hours
May have cheered the dreary mood;
When the votary turned to the world he had spurned,
And repined at the solitude.

Still do they blow 'mid the ruins below,
For fallen are fane and shrine,
And the moss has grown o'er the sculptured stone
Of an altar no more divine.

Still on the walls where the sunshine falls,
The ancient fruit-tree grows;
And o'er tablet and tomb, extends the bloom
Of many a wilding rose.

Fair though they be, yet they seemed to me
To mock the wreck below;
For mighty the tower, where the fragile flower
May now as in triumph blow.

Oh, foolish the thought, that my fancy brought;
More true and more wise to say,
That still thus doth spring, some gentle thing,

With its beauty to cheer decay.

Love Nursed By Solitude
Ay, surely it is here that Love should come,
And find, (if he may find on earth), a home;
Here cast off all the sorrow and the shame
That cling like shadows to his very name.

Young Love, thou art belied: they speak of thee,
And couple with thy mention misery;
Talk of the broken heart, the wasted bloom,
The spirit blighted, and the early tomb;
As if these waited on thy golden lot,
They blame thee for the faults which thou hast not.
Art thou to blame for that they bring on thee
The soil and weight of their mortality?
How can they hope that ever links will hold
Form'd, as they form them now, of the harsh gold?
Or worse than even this, how can they think
That vanity will bind the failing link?
How can they dream that thy sweet life will bear
Crowds', palaces', and cities' heartless air?
Where the lip smiles while the heart's desolate,
And courtesy lends its deep mask to hate;
Where looks and thoughts alike must feel the chain,
And nought of life is real but its pain;
Where the young spirit's high imaginings
Are scorn'd and cast away as idle things;
Where, think or feel, you are foredoom'd to be
A marvel and a sign for mockery;
Where none must wander from the beaten road,
All alike champ the bit, and feel the goad.
It is not made for thee, young Love! away
To where the green earth laughs to the clear day,
To the deep valley, where a thousand trees
Keep a green court for fairy revelries,
To some small island on a lonely lake,
Where only swans the diamond waters break,
Where the pines hang in silence oe'r the tide
And the stream gushes from the mountain side;
These, Love, are haunts for thee; where canst thou brood
With thy sweet wings furl'd but in Solitude.

Nymph And Zephyr: A Statuary Group
And the summer sun shone in the sky,
And the rose's whole life was in its sigh,
When her eyelids were kiss'd by a morning beam,
And the Nymph rose up from her moonlit dream;
For she had watch'd the midnight hour

Till her head had bow'd like a sleeping flower;
But now she had waken'd, and light and dew
Gave her morning freshness and morning hue,
Up she sprang, and away she fled
O'er the lithe grass stem and the blossom's head,
From the lillies' bells she dash'd not the spray,
For her feet were as light and as white as they.
Sudden upon her arm there shone
A gem with the hues of an Indian stone,
And she knew the insect bird whose wing
Is sacred to PSYCHE and to spring;
But scarce had her touch its captive prest
Ere another prisoner was on her breast,
And the Zephyr sought his prize again,
'No,' said the Nymph, thy search is vain:
And her golden hair from its braided yoke
Burst like the banner of hope as she spoke,
'And instead, fair boy, thou shalt moralize
Over the pleasure that from thee flies;
Then it is pleasure, for we possess
But in the search, not in the success.'

Juliet After The Masquerade
She left the festival, for it seem'd dim
Now that her eye no longer dwelt on him,
And sought her chamber, gazed, (then turn'd away),
Upon a mirror that before her lay,
Half fearing, half believing her sweet face
Would surely claim within his memory place.
The hour was late, and that night her light foot
Had been the constant echo of the lute;
Yet sought she not her pillow, the cool air
Came from the casement, and it lured her there.
The terrace was beneath, and the pale moon
Shone o'er the couch which she had press'd at noon,
Soft-lingering o'er some minstrel's love-lorn page,
Alas, tears are the poet's heritage!

She flung her on that couch, but not for sleep;
No, it was only that the wind might steep
Her fever'd lip in its delicious dew:
Her brow was burning, and aside she threw
Her cap and plume, and, loosen'd from its fold,
Came o'er her neck and face a shower of gold,
A thousand curls. It was a solitude
Made for young hearts in love's first dreaming mood:
Beneath the garden lay, fill'd with rose-trees
Whose sighings came like passion on the breeze.

Two graceful statues of the Parian stone

So finely shaped, that as the moonlight shone
The breath of life seem'd to their beauty given,
But less the life of earth than that of heaven.
'Twas Psyche and her boy-god, so divine
They turn'd the terrace to an idol shrine,
With its white vases and their summer share
Of flowers, like altars raised to that sweet pair.

And there the maiden leant, still in her ear
The whisper dwelt of that young cavalier;
It was no fancy, he had named the name
Of love, and at that thought her cheek grew flame:
It was the first time her young ear had heard
A lover's burning sigh, or silver word;
Her thoughts were all confusion, but most sweet,
Her heart beat high, but pleasant was its beat.

She murmur'd over many a snatch of song
That might to her own feelings now belong;
She thought upon old histories she had read,
And placed herself in each high heroine's stead,
Then woke her lute, oh! there is little known
Of music's power till aided by love's own.
And this is happiness: oh! love will last
When all that made it happiness is past,
When all its hopes are as the glittering toys
Time present offers, time to come destroys,
When they have been too often crush'd to earth,
For further blindness to their little worth,
When fond illusions have dropt one by one,
Like pearls from a rich carkanet, till none
Are left upon life's soil'd and naked string,
And this is all what time will ever bring.

 And that fair girl, what can the heart foresee
Of her young love, and of its destiny?
There is a white cloud o'er the moon, its form
Is very light, and yet there sleeps the storm;
It is an omen, it may tell the fate
Of love known all too soon, repented all too late.

Kate Kearney
Why doth the maiden turn away
From voice so sweet, and words so dear?
Why doth the maiden turn away
When love and flattery woo her ear?
And rarely that enchanted twain
Whisper in woman's ear in vain.
Why doth the maiden leave the hall?
No face is fair as hers is fair,

No step has such a fairy fall,
No azure eyes like hers are there.

The maiden seeks her lonely bower,
Although her father's guests are met;
She knows it is the midnight hour,
She knows the first pale star is set,
And now the silver moon-beams wake
The spirits of the haunted Lake.
The waves take rainbow hues, and now
The shining train are gliding by,
Their chieftain lifts his glorious brow,
The maiden meets his lingering eye.

The glittering shapes melt into night;
Another look, their chief is gone,
And chill and gray comes morning's light,
And clear and cold the Lake flows on;
Close, close the casement, not for sleep,
Over such visions eyes but weep.

How many share such destiny,
How many, lured by fancy's beam,
Ask the impossible to be,
And pine, the victims of a dream.

Hebe

Youth! thou art a lovely time,
With thy wild and dreaming eyes;
Looking onwards to their prime,
Coloured by their April skies,
Yet I do not wish for thee,
Pass, oh! quickly pass from me.

Thou hast all too much unrest,
Haunted by vain hopes and fears;
Though thy cheeks with smiles be drest,
Yet that cheek is wet with tears.
Bitter are the frequent showers,
Falling in thy sunny hours.

Let my heart grow calm and cold,
Calm to sorrow, cold to love;
Let affections loose their hold,
Let my spirit look above.
I am weary—youth pass on.
All thy dearest gifts are gone.

She in whose sweet form the Greek
Bade his loveliest vision dwell;

She of yon bright cup and cheek,
From her native heaven fell:
Type of what may never last,
Soon the heaven of youth is past.

Oh! farewell—for never more
Can thy dreams again be mine;
Hope and truth and faith are o'er,
And the heart which was their shrine
Has no boon of thee to seek,
Asking but to rest or break.

Cupid And Swallows Flying From Winter. By Dagley
'We fly from the cold.'

Away, away, o'er land and sea,
This is now no home for me;
My light wings may never bear
Northern cloud or winter air.
Murky shades are gathering fast,
Sleet and snow are on the blast,
Trees from which the leaves are fled,
Flowers whose very roots are dead,
Grass of its green blade bereft,
These are all that now are left.
 Linger here another day,
I shall be as sad as they;
My companions fly with spring,
I too must be on the wing.

Where are the sweet gales whose song
Wont to waft my darts along?
Scented airs! oh, not like these,
Rough as they which sweep the seas;
But those sighs of rose which bring
Incense from their wandering.
Where are the bright flowers that kept
Guard around me while I slept?

Where the sunny eyes whose beams
Waken'd me from my soft dreams?
These are with the swallows gone,
Beauty's heart is chill'd to stone.

Oh! for some sweet southern clime,
Where 'tis ever summer time,
Where, if blossoms fall, their tomb
Is amid new birth of bloom,
Where green leaves are ever springing,
Where the lark is always singing,

One of those bright isles which lie
Fair beneath an azure sky,
Isles of cinnamon and spice,
Shadow each of Paradise,
Where the flowers shine with dyes,
Tinted bright from the sun-rise,
Where the birds which drink their dew,
Wave wings of yet brighter hue,
And each river's course is roll'd
Over bed of pearl and gold!

Oh! for those lime-scented groves
Where the Spanish lover roves,
Tuning to the western star,
His soft song and light guitar,
Where the dark hair'd girls are dancing,
Fairies in the moonlight glancing,
With pencill'd brows, and radiant eyes,
Like their planet-lighted skies!
Or those clear Italian lakes
Where the silver cygnet makes
Its soft nest of leaf and flower,
A white lily for its bower!

Each of these a home would be,
Fit for beauty and for me:
I must seek their happier sphere
While the Winter lords it here.

Fairies On The Sea Shore. By Howard
FIRST FAIRY.
My home and haunt are in every leaf,
Whose life is a summer day, bright and brief,
I live in the depths of the tulip's bower,
I wear a wreath of the cistus flower,
I drink the dew of the blue harebell,
I know the breath of the violet well,
The white and the azure violet;
But I know not which is the sweetest yet,
I have kiss'd the cheek of the rose;
I have watch'd the lily unclose,
My silver mine is the almond tree,
Who will come dwell with flower and me?

CHORUS OF FAIRIES.
Dance we our round, 'tis a summer night,
And our steps are led by the glow-worms' light.

SECOND FAIRY.
My dwelling is in the serpentine

Of the rainbow's colour'd line,
See how its rose and amber clings
To the many hues of my radiant wings;
Mine is the step that bids the earth
Give to the iris flower its birth,
And mine the golden cup to hide,
Where the last faint hue of the rainbow died.
Search the depths of an Indian mine,
Where are the colours to match with mine?

CHORUS.
Dance we round, for the gale is bringing
Songs the summer rose is singing.

THIRD FAIRY.
I float on the breath of a minstrel's lute,
Or the wandering sounds of a distant flute,
Linger I over the tones that swell
From the pink-vein'd chords of an ocean-shell;
I love the sky-lark's morning hymn,
Or the nightingale heard at the twilight dim,
The echo, the fountain's melody,
These, oh! these are the spells for me!

CHORUS.
Hail to the summer night of June;
See! yonder has risen our ladye moon.

FOURTH SPIRIT.
My palace is in the coral cave
Set with spars by the ocean wave;
Would ye have gems, then seek them there,
There found I the pearls that bind my hair.
I and the wind together can roam
Over the green waves and their white foam,
See, I have got this silver shell,
Mark how my breath will its smallness swell,
For the Nautilus is my boat
In which I over the waters float,
The moon is shining over the sea,
Who is there will come sail with me?

CHORUS OF FAIRIES.
Our noontide sleep is on leaf and flower,
Our revels are held in a moonlit hour,
What is there sweet, what is there fair,
And we are not the dwellers there?
Dance we round, for the morning light,
Will put us and our glow-worm lamps to flight!

Love, Hope And Beauty
Love may be increased by fears,
May be fanned with sighs,
Nursed by fancies, fed by doubts;
But without Hope it dies!
As in the far Indian isles
Dies the young cocoa tree,
Unless within the pleasant shade
Of the parent plant it be;
So Love may spring up at first
Lighted at Beauty's eyes:
But Beauty is not all its life,
For without Hope it dies.

New Year's Eve
There is no change upon the air,
No record in the sky:
No pall-like storm comes forth to shroud
The year about to die.

A few light clouds are on the heaven,
A few far stars are bright;
And the pale moon shines as she shines
On many a common night.

Ah, not in heaven, but upon earth,
Are signs of change exprest;
The closing year has left its mark
On human brow and breast.

How much goes with it to the grave
Of life's most precious things?
Methinks each year dies on a pyre,
Like the Assyrian kings.

Affections, friendships, confidence,
There's not a year hath died
But all these treasures of the heart
Lie with it side by side.

The wheels of time work heavily;
We marvel day by day
To see how from the chain of life
The gilding wears away.

Sad the mere change of fortune's chance,
And sad the friend unkind;
But what has sadness like the change
That in ourselves we find?

I've wept my castle in the dust,
Wept o'er an altered brow;
'Tis far worse murmuring o'er those tears,
"Would I could weep them now!"

O, for mine early confidence,
Which like that graceful tree
Bent cordial, as if each approach
Could but in kindness be!

Then was the time the fairy Hope
My future fortune told,
Or Youth, the alchymist, that turned

Home

I Left my home; 'twas in a little vale
Sheltered from snow-storms by the stately pines;
A small clear river wandered quietly,
Its smooth waves only cut by the light barks
Of fishers, and but darkened by the shade
The willows flung, when to the southern wind
They threw their long green tresses. On the slope
Were five or six white cottages, whose roofs
Reached not to the laburnum's height, whose boughs
Shook over them bright showers of golden bloom.
Sweet silence reigned around:—no other sound
Came on the air, than when the shepherd made
The reed-pipe rudely musical, or notes
From the wild birds, or children in their play
Sending forth shouts of laughter. Strangers come
Rarely or never near the lonely place.....
I went into far countries. Years passed by,

But still that vale in silent beauty dwelt
Within my memory. Home I came at last.
I stood upon a mountain height, and looked
Into the vale below; and smoke arose,
And heavy sounds; and through the thick dim air
Shot blackened turrets, and brick walls, and roofs
Of the red tile. I entered in the streets:
There were ten thousand hurrying to and fro;
And masted vessels stood upon the river,
And barges sullied the once dew-clear stream:
Where were the willows, where the cottages?
I sought my home; I sought, and found a city,
Alas! for the green valley!

The Battle Field

He sleeps-the night wind o'er the battle-field

Is gently sighing;
Gently, though each breeze bear away
Life from the dying.

He sleeps,-though his dear and early friend
A corpse lies by him;
Though the ravening vulture and screaming crow
Are hovering nigh him.

He sleeps,-where blood has been poured like rain,
Another field before him:
And he sleeps as calm as his mother's eyes
Were watching o'er him.

To-morrow that youthful victor's name
Will be proudly given,
By the trumpet's voice, and the soldier's shout,
To the winds of heaven.

Yet life, how pitiful and how mean,
Thy noblest story;
When the high excitement of victory,
The fullness of glory,

Nor the sorrow felt for the friend of his youth,
Whose corpse he is keeping,
Can give his human weakness force
To keep from sleeping.

And this is the sum of our mortal state,
The hopes we number,
Feverish, waking, danger, death,
And listless slumber.

The Female Convict

She shrank from all, and her silent mood
Made her wish only for solitude:
Her eye sought the ground, as it could not brook,
For innermost shame, on another's to look;
And the cheerings of comfort fell on her ear
Like deadliest words, that were curses to hear!

She still was young, and she had been fair;
But weather-stains, hunger, toil, and care,
That frost and fever that wear the heart,
Had made the colours of youth depart
From the sallow cheek, save over it came
The burning flush of the spirit's shame.

They were sailing o'er the salt sea-foam,

Far from her country, far from her home;
And all she had left for her friends to keep
Was a name to hide, and a memory to weep!
And her future held forth but the felon's lot,
To live forsaken—to die forgot!
She could not weep, and she could not pray,
But she wasted and withered from day to day,
Till you might have counted each sunken vein,
When her wrist was prest by the iron chain;
And sometimes I thought her large dark eye
Had the glisten of red insanity.

She called me once to her sleeping place,
A strange, wild look was upon her face,
Her eye flashed over her cheek so white,
Like a gravestone seen in the pale moonlight,
And she spoke in a low, unearthly tone—
The sound from mine ear hath never gone!"
I had last night the loveliest dream:
My own land shone in the summer beam,
I saw the fields of the golden grain,
I heard the reaper's harvest strain;
There stood on the hills the green pine tree,
And the thrush and the lark sang merrily.
A long and a weary way I had come;
But I stopped, methought, by mine own sweet home,

I stood by the hearth, and my father sat there,
With pale, thin face, and snow-white hair!
The Bible lay open upon his knee,
But he closed the book to welcome me.
He led me next where my mother lay,
And together we knelt by her grave to pray,
And heard a hymn it was heaven to hear,
For it echoed one to my young days dear.
This dream has waked feelings long, long since fled,
And hopes which I deemed in my heart were dead!
We have not spoken, but still I have hung
On the northern accents that dwell on thy tongue
To me they are music, to me they recall
The things long hidden by Memory's pall!
Take this long curl of yellow hair,
And give it my father, and tell him my prayer,
My dying prayer, was for him."....
Next day
Upon the deck a coffin lay;
They raised it up, and like a dirge
The heavy gale swept o'er the surge;
The corpse was cast to the wind and wave—
The convict has found in the green sea a grave.

Song Of The Hunter's Bride

Another day—another day—
And yet he comes not nigh;
I look amid the dim blue hills,
Yet nothing meets mine eye.

I hear the rush of mountain streams
Upon the echoes borne;
I hear the singing of the birds,
But not my hunter's horn.

The eagle sails in darkness past,
The watchful chamois bounds;
But what I look for comes not near,
My Ulric's hawk and hounds.

Three times I thus have watched the snow
Grow crimson with the stain,
The setting sun threw o'er the rock,
And I have watched in vain.

I love to see the graceful bow
Across his shoulder slung,
I love to see the golden horn
Beside his baldric hung.

I love his dark hounds, and I love
His falcon's sweeping flight;
I love to see his manly cheek
With mountain colors bright.

I've waited patiently, but now
Would that the chase was o'er:
Well may he love the hunter's toil,
But he should love me more.

Why stays he thus? he would be here,
If his love equalled mine;
Methinks had I one fond caged dove,
I would not let it pine.

But, hark! what are those ringing steps
That up the valley come?
I see his hounds—I see himself
My Ulric, welcome home!

Love

She prest her slight hand to her brow, or pain
Or bitter thoughts were passing there. The room

Had no light but that from the fireside,
Which showed, then hid her face. How very pale
It looked, when over it the glimmer shone!
Is not the rose companion of the spring?
Then wherefore has the red-leaved flower forgotten
Her cheek? The tears stood in her large dark eyes
Her beautiful dark eyes—like hyacinth stars,
When shines their shadowy glory through the dew
That summer nights have wept; she felt them not,
Her heart was far away! Her fragile form,
Like the young willow when for the first time
The wind sweeps o'er it rudely, had not lost
Its own peculiar grace; but it was bowed
By sickness, or by worse than sickness—sorrow!
And this is Love!—O! why should woman love;
Wasting her dearest feelings, till health, hope,
Happiness, are but things of which henceforth
She'll only know the name? Her heart is seared:
A sweet light has been thrown upon its life,
To make its darkness the more terrible.
And this is Love!

When Should Lovers Breathe Their Vows?
When should lovers breathe their vows?
When should ladies hear them?
When the dew is on the boughs,
When none else are near them;
When the moon shines cold and pale,
When the birds are sleeping,
When no voice is on the gale,
When the rose is weeping;
When the stars are bright on high
Like hopes in young Love's dreaming,

And glancing round the light clouds fly,
Like soft fears to shade their beaming.
The fairest smiles are those that live
On the brow by starlight wreathing;
And the lips their richest incense give
When the sigh is at midnight breathing.
O, softest is the cheek's love-ray
When seen by moonlight hours;
Other roses seek the day,
But blushes are night-flowers.
O, when the moon and stars are bright,
When the dew-drops glisten,
Then their vows should lovers plight,
Then should ladies listen!

The Lost Star

A light is gone from yonder sky,
A star has left its sphere;
The beautiful—and do they die
In yon bright world as here?
Will that star leave a lonely place,
A darkness on the night?
No; few will miss its lovely face,
And none will think heaven less bright!

What wert thou star of? vanished one,
What mystery was thine?
Thy beauty from the east is gone:
What was thy sway and sign?
Wert thou the star of opening youth?
And is it then for thee,
Its frank glad thoughts, its stainless truth,
So early cease to be?

Of hope—and was it to express
How soon hope sinks in shade;
Or else of human loveliness,
In sign how it will fade? How was thy dying—like the song,
In music to the last,
An echo flung the winds among,
And then for ever past?

Or didst thou sink as stars whose light
The fair moon renders vain?
The rest shone forth the next dark night,
Thou didst not shine again.
Didst thou fade gradual from the time
The first great curse was hurled,
Till lost in sorrow and in crime,
Star of our early world?

Forgotten and departed star!
A thousand glories shine
Round the blue midnight's regal car,
Who then remembers thine?
Save when some mournful bard like me
Dreams over beauty gone,
And in the fate that waited thee,
Reads what will be his own.

Glencoe

Lay by the harp, sing not that song,
Although so very sweet;
It is the song of other years,
For thee and me unmeet.

Thy head is pillowed on my arm,
Thy heart beats close to mine;
Methinks it were unjust to heaven,
If we should now repine.

I must not weep, you must not sing
That thrilling song again,
I dare not think upon the time
When last I heard that strain.

It was a silent summer eve:
We stood by the hill-side,
And we could see my ship afar
Breasting the ocean tide.

Around us grew the graceful larch,
A calm blue sky above,
Beneath were little cottages,
The homes of peace and love.

Thy harp was by thee then, as now,
One hand in mine was laid;
The other, wandering' mid the chords,
A soothing music made:

Just two or three sweet chords, that seemed
An echo of thy tone,
The cushat's song was on the wind,
And mingled with thine own.

I looked upon the vale beneath.
I looked on thy sweet face;
I thought how dear, this voyage o'er,
Would be my resting place.

We parted; but I kept thy kiss,
Thy last one, and its sigh,
As safely as the stars are kept
In yonder azure sky.

Again I stood by that hill-side,
And scarce I knew the place,
For fire, and blood, and death, had left
On everything their trace.

The lake was covered o'er with weeds,
Choked was our little rill,
There was no sign of corn or grass,
The cushat's song was still:

Burnt to the dust, an ashy heap
Was every cottage round;
I listened but I could not hear
One single human sound:

I spoke, and only my own words
Were echoed from the hill;
I sat me down to weep, and curse
The hand that wrought this ill.

We met again by miracle:
Thou wert another one
Saved from this work of sin and death,
I was not quite alone.

And then I heard the evil tale
Of guilt and suffering,
Till I prayed the curse of God might fall
On the false-hearted king.

I will not think on this, for thou
Art saved, and saved for me!
And gallantly my little bark
Cuts through the moonlight sea.

There's not a shadow in the sky,
The waves are bright below;
I must not, on so sweet a night,
Think upon dark Glencoe.

If thought were vengeance, then its thought
A ceaseless fire should be,
Burning by day, burning by night,
Kept like a thought of thee.

But I am powerless and must flee;
That e'er a time should come,
When we should shun our own sweet land,
And seek another home!

This must not be, yon soft moonlight
Falls on my heart like balm;
The waves are still, the air is hushed,
And I too will be calm.
Away! we seek another land
Of hope, stars, flowers, sunshine;
I shall forget the dark green hills
Of that which once was mine!

The Change

Thy features do not bear the light
They wore in happier days;
Though still there may be much to love,
There's little left to praise.

The rose has faded from thy cheek
There's scarce a blush left now;
And there's a dark and weary sign
Upon thine altered brow.

Thy raven hair is dashed with gray,
Thine eyes are dim with tears;
And care, before thy youth is past,
Has done the work of years.

Beautiful wreck! for still thy face
Though changed, is very fair;
Like beauty's moonlight, left to show
Her morning sun was there.

Come, here are friends and festival,
Recall thine early smile;
And wear yon wreath, whose glad red rose
Will lend its bloom awhile.

Come, take thy lute, and sing again
The song you used to sing
The birdlike song: See, though unused,
The lute has every string.

What, doth thy hand forget the lute?
Thy brow reject the wreath?
Alas! whate'er the change above,
There's more of change beneath?

The smile may come, the smile may go,
The blush shineand depart;
But farewell when their sense is quenched
Within the breaking heart.

And such is thine: 'tis vain to seek
The shades of past delight:
Fling down the wreath, and break the lute;
They mock our souls to-night.

Can You Forget Me?
Can you forget me? I who have so cherished
The veriest trifle that was memory's link;
The roses that you gave me, although perished,
Were precious in my sight; they made me think.

You took them in their scentless beauty stooping
From the warm shelter of the garden wall;
Autumn, while into languid winter drooping,
Gave its last blossoms, opening but to fall.
Can you forget them?

Can you forget me? I am not relying
On plighted vows—alas! I know their worth:
Man's faith to woman is a trifle, dying
Upon the very breath that gave it birth.
But I remember hours of quiet gladness,
When, if the heart had truth, it spoke it then,
When thoughts would sometimes take a tone of sadness,
And then unconsciously grow glad again.
Can you forget them?

Can you forget me? My whole soul was blended;
At least it sought to blend itself with thine;
My life's whole purpose, winning thee, seemed ended;
Thou wert my heart's sweet home—my spirit's shrine
Can you forget me? when the firelight burning,
Flung sudden gleams around the quiet room,
How would thy words, to long past moments turning,
Trust me with thoughts soft as the shadowy gloom!
Can you forget them?

There is no truth in love, whate'er its seeming,
And heaven itself could scarcely seem more true
Sadly have I awakened from the dreaming,
Whose charmed slumber—false one! was of you.
I gave mine inmost being to thy keeping
I had no thought I did not seek to share;
Feelings that hushed within my soul were sleeping,
Waked into voice, to trust them to thy care.
Can you forget them?

Can you forget me? This is vainly tasking
The faithless heart where I, alas! am not.
Too well I know the idleness of asking—
The misery-of why am I forgot?
The happy hours that I have passed while kneeling
Half slave, half child, to gaze upon thy face.
—But what to thee this passionate appealing
Let my heart break-it is a common case.
You have forgotten me.

Expectation
She looked from out the window
With long and asking gaze,
From the gold-clear light of morning

To the twilight's purple haze.
Cold and pale the planets shone,
Still the girl kept gazing on.
From her white and weary forehead
Droopeth the dark hair,
Heavy with the dews of evening,
Heavier with her care;
Falling as the shadows fall,
Till flung round her like a pall.

When from the carved lattice
First she leant to look,
Her bright face was written
Like some pleasant book
Her warm cheek the red air quaffed,
And her eyes looked out and laughed.
She is leaning back now languid,
And her cheek is white;
Only on the drooping eyelash
Glistens tearful light.
Color, sunshine hours are gone,
Yet the lady watches on.

Human heart, this history
Is thy faded lot;
Even such thy watching,
For what cometh not,
Till with anxious waiting dull,
Round thee fades the beautiful,
Still thou seekest on, though weary,
Seeking still in vain:
Daylight deepens into twilight,
What has been thy gain?
Death and night are closing round,
All that thou hast sought unfound.

The Lake Of Como
Again I am beside the lake,
The lonely lake, which used to be
The wide world of the beating heart,
When I was, love, with thee.

I see the quiet evening lights
Amid the distant mountains shine;
I hear the music of a lute;
It used to come from thine.

How can another sing the song,
The sweet sad song that was thine own?
It is alike, yet not the same;

It has not caught thy tone.

Ah, never other lip may catch
The sweetness round thine own that clung;
To me there is a tone unheard,
There is a chord unstrung.

Thou loveliest lake, I sought thy shores,
That dreams from other days might cast
The presence elsewhere sought in vain,
The presence of the past.

I find the folly of the search,
Thou bringest but half the past again;
My pleasure calling faintly back
Too vividly my pain.

Too real the memories that haunt
The purple shadows round thy brink
I only asked of thee to dream,
I did not ask to think.

False beauty haunting still my heart,
Though long since from that heart removed;
These waves but tell me how thou wert
Too well and vainly loved.

Fair lake, it is all vain to seek
The influence of thy lonely shore
I ask of thee for hope and love
They come to me no more.

The Pirate's Song

To the mast nail our flag, it is dark as the grave,
Or the death which it bears while it sweeps o'er the wave.
Let our deck clear for action, our guns be prepared;
Be the boarding-axe sharpened, the cimetar bared;
Set the canisters ready, and then bring to me,
For the last of my duties, the powder-room key.
It shall never be lowered, the black flag we bear;
If the sea be denied us, we sweep through the air.

Unshared have we left our last victory's prey;
It is mine to divide it, and yours to obey.
There are shawls that might suit a sultana's white neck,
And pearls that are fair as the arms they will deck:
There are flasks which, unseal them, the air will disclose
Diametta's fair summer, the home of the rose.
I claim not a portion; I ask but as mine,
'Tis to drink to our victory—one cup of red wine.

Some fight,'tis for riches; some fight, 'tis for fame;
The first, I despise, and the last is a name.
I fight, 'tis for vengeance. I love to see flow,
At the stroke of my sabre, the life of my foe.
I strike for the memory of long vanished years;
I only shed blood, where another sheds tears.
I come, as the lightning comes red from above,
O'er the race that I loathe, to the battle I love.

The Widow's Mite

It is the fruit of waking hours
When others are asleep,
When moaning round the low thatched roof
The winds of winter creep.

It is the fruit of summer days
Passed in a gloomy room,
When others are abroad to taste
The pleasant morning bloom.

'Tis given from a scanty store,
And missed while it is given;
'Tis given—for the claims of earth
Are less than those of heaven.

Few save the poor feel for the poor;
The rich know not how hard
It is to be of needful food
And needful rest debarred.

Their paths are paths of plenteousness;
They sleep on silk and down,
And never think how heavily
The weary head lies down.

They know not of the scanty meal
With small pale faces round;
No fire upon the cold, damp hearth,
When snow is on the ground.

They never by their window sit,
And see the gay pass by;
Yet take their weary work again,
Though with a mournful eye.

The rich, they give—they miss it not
A blessing cannot be
Like that which rests, thou widowed one,
Upon thy gift and thee!

Cottage Courtship

Now, out upon this smiling,
No smile shall meet his sight;
And a word of gay reviling
Is all he'll hear to-night;
For he'll hold my smiles too lightly,
If he always sees me smile;
He'll think they shine more brightly,
When I have frowned awhile

'Tis not kindness keeps a lover,
He must feel the chain he wears
All the sweet enchantment's over,
When he has no anxious cares.
The heart would seem too common,
If he thought that heart his own;
Ah! the empire of a woman
Is still in the unknown.

Let change without a reason,
Make him never feel secure;
For it is an April season
That a lover must endure.
They are all of them so faithless,
Their torment is your gain;
Would you keep your own heart scathless,
Be the one to give the pain.

The Phantom

I come from my home in the depth of the sea,
I come that thy dreams may be haunted by me;
Not as we parted, the rose on my brow,
But shadowy, silent, I visit thee now.
The time of our parting was when the moon shone,
Of all heaven's daughters the loveliest one;
No cloud in her presence, no star at her side,
She smiled on her mirror and vassal, the tide.

Unbroken its silver, undreamed of its swell,
There was hope, and not fear, in our midnight farewell;
While drooping around were the wings white and wild,
Of the ship that was sleeping, as slumbers a child.
I turned to look from thee, to look on the bower,
Which thou hast been training in sunshine and shower;
So thick were the green leaves, the sun and the rain
Sought to pierce through the shelter from summer in vain.

It was not its ash-tree, the home of the wren,

And the haunt of the bee, I was thinking of then;
Nor yet of the violets, sweet on the air,
But I thought of the true love who planted them there.
I come to thee now, my long hair on the gale,
It is wreathed with no red rose, is bound with no veil,
It is dark with the sea damps, and wet with the spray,
The gold of its auburn has long past away.

And dark is the cavern wherein I have slept,
There the seal and the dolphin their vigil have kept;
And the roof is incrusted with white coral cells,
Wherein the strange insect that buildeth them dwells.
There is life in the shells that are strewed o'er the sands,
Not filled but with music as on our own strands;
Around me are whitening the bones of the dead,
And a starfish has grown to the rock overhead.

Sometimes a vast shadow goes darkly along,
The shark or the sword-fish, the fearful and strong:
There is fear in the eyes that are glaring around,
As they pass like the spectres of death without sound:
Over rocks, without summer, the dull sea-weeds trail,
And the blossoms that hang there are scentless and pale;
Amid their dark garlands, the water-snakes glide,
And the sponge, like the moss, gathers thick at their side.

O! would that the sunshine could fall on my grave,
That the wild flower and willow could over it wave;
O! would that the daisies grew over my sleep,
That the tears of the morning could over me weep.
Thou art pale 'mid the dreams, I shall trouble no more,
The sorrow that kept me from slumber is o'er;
To the depths of the ocean in peace I depart,
For I still have a grave greener far in thy heart!

Dirge

Lay her in the gentle earth,
Where the summer maketh mirth;
Where young violets have birth;
Where the lily bendeth.
Lay her there, the lovely one!
With the rose, her funeral stone;
And for tears, such showers alone
As the rain of April lendeth.

From the midnight's quiet hour
Will come dews of holy power,
O'er the sweetest human flower
That was ever loved.
But she was too fair and dear

For our troubled pathway here;
Heaven, that was her natural sphere,
Has its own removed.

The Legacy Of The Lute

Come take the lute—the lute I loved
'Tis all I have to offer thee;
And may it be less fatal gift
Than it has ever been to me.
My sigh yet lingers on the strings,
The strings I have not heart to break:
Wilt thou not, dearest! keep the lute
For mine—for the departed's sake?
But, pray thee, do not wake that lute;

Leave it upon the cypress tree;
I would have crushed its charmed chords,
But they so oft were strung to thee.
The minstrel-lute! O, touch it not,
Or weary destiny is thine!
Thy life a twilight's haunted dream
Thou, victim, at an idol's shrine.

Thy breath but lives on others' lips
Thy hope, a thing beyond the grave,
Thy heart, bare to the vulture's beak
Thyself a bound and bartered slave.
And yet a dangerous charm o'er all,
A bright but ignis—fatuus flame.
Luring thee with a show of power,
Dazzling thee with a blaze of flame.

It is to waste on careless hearts
The throbbing music of thine own
 To speak love's burning words, yet be
Alone—ay, utterly alone.
I sought to fling my laure
I wreath Away upon the autumn wind:
In vain, 'twas like those poisoned crowns
Thou may'st not from the brow unbind.

Predestined from my birth to feed
On dreams, yet watch those dreams depart,
To bear through life—to feel in death
A burning and a broken heart.
Then hang it on the cypress bough,
The minstrel-lute I leave to thee;
And be it only for the wind
To wake its mournful dirge for me.

www.ingramcontent.com/pod-product-compliance
Lightning Source LLC
Chambersburg PA
CBHW060144050426
42448CB00010B/2288